Falling

A Couple's Memoir of Medicine, Mountains, and
Multiple Sclerosis

Clint Pearson & Ursula Pearson

[signatures]

Aberdeen Bay

Atlanta - Beijing - Harbin - Washington, D.C.

Aberdeen Bay
Published by Aberdeen Bay, an imprint of Champion Writers.
www.aberdeenbay.com

PUBLISHER'S NOTE

Aberdeen Bay is not responsible for the accuracy of this
book--including but not limited to events, people, dates, and
locations.

International Standard Book Number
ISBN-13: 978-1-60830-012-9
ISBN-10: 1-60830-012-9

Printed in the United States of America.

A Note from the Authors

While our story is true and the incidents we describe did indeed take place, as a safeguard for their privacy we have chosen to refer to patients, patients' family members, and other physicians and caregivers by names other than their real ones. In the same way, we have chosen to refer to specific hospitals, clinics, and other such facilities in general terms with the intent that no particular institution can be identified.

Acknowledgments

Special thanks to our loving family: Veda Francis, Marcia and Othel Pearson, Rudy Francis, Charmaigne Menn, Andora Joshua, Shirley Lewis, Beverly Pather, Lance Pearson, Kelly Pearson, and Kit Pearson.
Also special thanks to Jim and Nancy Wilson for their encouragement and support, Patricia Benzon for her unyielding support and honesty, Margie Godwyn and Betsy White for their critical expertise.

Foreword

Recently, my husband and I visited our son and his family. Before breakfast I watched as our daughter-in-law began the process of getting our son out of bed, showered, dressed, and into his wheelchair. Our son, a physician, has battled MS for twenty-eight years. We have seen him go from running cross-country to using a cane, then a walker, then a power chair. On this particular morning, he was stiffer and weaker than usual because he was recovering from pneumonia.

My husband could have simply lifted our son and placed him in his chair, but our son and his wife wanted to do it their way, a series of lifts, pivots, holds, pushes, pulls, and hugs. Engaged in what they were doing, they seemed unaware of my presence. Their six-year-old twins got ready for school as they would on any other day. Our son stood and held onto a bar while our daughter-in-law pulled up his pants. Then she maneuvered him into the power chair, put on his socks and shoes, and struggled to place his feet on the footrests. Finally she pulled his shirt over his head and brushed his hair. When they had completed their morning routine, our son lifted his hand for a high-five. Our daughter-in-law slapped her palm against his, and they said in unison, "Yes!"

Marcia Pearson

Dedication

For all the patients whose stories are a part of this book, may you explore many new and wondrous mountains. For Jasmine and Denali whose stories are just beginning, may you do the same.

Falling

CHAPTER ONE

Birth

Life is either a daring adventure or nothing.
-- Helen Keller

Clint

"I'm not stopping." I snarled the words and raised
my face, feeling water drip from my chin. The only reply was
the brook's quiet gurgle and the sweep of wind in the cedars.
I looked up the gully, glaring at the trees and mountains that
blocked my view of Homer's Nose, a prominent but little-known
peak in the Sierra Nevada. For years I had gazed at the Nose,
hiked beneath it, marveled at it, and ached to stand on top with
my chest heaving.

Then one day in June of 1984, when I was eighteen
years old, the fantasy tore from me like an irrepressible laugh,
a soft chuckle at first, then louder, less discrete, and finally
raucous, delirious laughter, disturbing and wild. Senselessly,
I chose to climb without food, water, or a map. A well-worn
pack, a sleeping bag, and a new Old Timer knife were my only
companions, and after three miles on a dusty trail, I found
myself looking toward Homer's Nose and growling at a stream
that tempted me to drink too much and rest too long.

"Get your ass in gear." I stood, pulled on my pack, and
bounded forward as if at the crack of a starting gun. A local
track star, I measured worth rigidly and intolerantly, as would a
stopwatch.

Straightaway, the trail started to climb and challenged
me with an endless supply of switchbacks. I began to labor,
blowing through pursed lips but smiling at the strain. I told

myself to keep working and was only vaguely aware of warmth building on the backs of my heels, compliments of my new boots.

From time to time, I caught glimpses of the stony smoothness of Homer's Nose, its bold rounded contour topping the skyline more like a baby's butt than a snout. Those glimpses fueled my adrenaline, driving my legs faster and faster, until soon I was caught up in the motion, mesmerized by the rhythm and the nonstop, in-and-out rush of air.

Doubt flew away then, common sense as well. I simply could not stop, any more than a laboring woman could halt her birth contractions. The infant was coming, butt-first with a ways to go, but given enough time and effort, I was certain to deliver myself upon the summit.

Hours went by and the trail veered east away from Homer's Nose. That wouldn't do for me, so I abandoned it, climbing directly up the mountain's face. As hiking became climbing that became hand-over-hand climbing, I stuck to my course without pause, without thought. My heels burned, my mouth felt parched, but when I topped the ridge I grinned, feeling wonderfully wild.

It was at that glorious moment, without warning, that my vision blurred, forcing me to stop. I closed my eyes and shook my head emphatically.

"No way, no repeat performance."

I fought to slow my breathing and blinked several times at the memory. Two years earlier after an intense workout on the track, my vision had blurred and then doubled with offset images that shifted and gyrated. For several weeks thereafter as I negotiated the corridors at Porterville High, I had to tilt my head and touch the walls to stay on my feet. Walking became difficult, running impossible, and although Dr. Taylor had nodded while listening to my story, afterward he scratched his gray beard, then handed me a slip for blood tests and a brain scan.

I got the diagnosis of multiple sclerosis from a young neurologist who looked more like an accountant than a physician. He delivered the fateful news as blandly as if he'd said how much I owed on my taxes. Then he cleared his throat,

shuffled some papers, and handed me a prescription for
prednisone. He'd offered few answers, no cause, no explanation.
I shook my head, remembering. "Stupid son of a bitch couldn't
diagnose crap."

"What the . . ." I jumped away from a fallen log, swiping
and slapping at scores of ants crawling up my pant leg. I got
most of them, and soon I was on the backside of the mountain,
moving nearer the Nose when abruptly I stopped and stared.

There sprawling across the mountainside like an
unkempt hedge was a community of bush chinquapin, far
thicker than usual. Their branches stretched and intertwined in
knotty tangles, creating dark and tortuous passageways that ran
low to the ground and admitted only the smallest of animals. I
searched for a gap, some weakness in the foliage. Going around
seemed unthinkable, for it would cost me much of the elevation
I'd gained. Going over the bushes seemed impossible as well,
but I decided to try it and made surprisingly steady headway.

Twice I fell through the branches, catching an arm on the
first occasion, scratching my back on the second, but both times,
I managed to twist and bully my body back on top. Slowly, in
halting stop-starts, I kept up my awkward balancing act. When I
thought how absurd I must look, I laughed out loud, but the next
wiry branch snapped off my chuckle. At the end, I raised my
arms, let out a growl, even spat on the bushes.

An hour later, so near Homer's Nose that success felt
assured, I became aware of my thirst. A brief but frenzied search
brought me to a fern-lined spring where I fell to the ground,
laughing like a child. I plunged my face, nose, and hands into the
icy water and drank until they ached. Then I stood, flicking and
rubbing the water from my hands, and screamed with a joyous
pain. The sound raced across the mountainside, reverberated
through the pines, and sent a red-tailed hawk into flight.

Refreshed, I was ready to go for the final push, and
despite my throbbing heels, I stormed up the backside of the
Nose without rest. Close to the top, the rocky surface flattened
out and the sky widened before me, blissful and glowing with an
orange sunset.

I walked to the edge of the rock, squinting from the

Falling

sunset's glare. A cold gust slapped my face, but I didn't mind. I simply raised my arms and continued staring across the immense expanse. In time, I lowered my arms, and the air changed from cool to cold as the sun disappeared.

A shiver broke my reverie, but I moved slowly to unroll my sleeping bag and to remove my boots. Huge blisters had formed on the backs of my heels and had long since ruptured, leaving flaps of wet pink skin that hung below my Achilles tendons like tattered tissue paper. Released from the confines of my boots, my heels throbbed, but I had no remedy for it. I simply crawled into my sleeping bag and tried to sleep.

My stomach rumbled, but it didn't seem to matter. The struggle was over, the baby born, or so I thought. Yet, throughout the night, I slept restlessly and didn't dream of winning. Instead, I saw myself starting a race. The gun sounded, and the crowd gave a brief cheer, but when I looked, the stadium was vacant except for two small children eating ice cream. Then someone whispered my name, and I turned but saw only empty bleachers. When I turned back, the children were gone, and although the arena was relatively quiet, the wind blew through the stands, rattling the railings and whistling strange admonitions that I couldn't comprehend.

I awoke hungry, a curious sensation, not particularly painful but annoying, like an itchy bug bite. It was still dark but with a faint lightening of the sky that faded the stars. Not ready to face the cold air, I stayed nestled in my bag for a long time.

At last, I pushed out of the bag and made ready to leave, but my initial attempt at putting on my boots brought yelps of pain, and I had to fight the urge to throw my boots off the mountain. Even after I got them on and laced them with a generous supply of cursing, the swear words kept coming as I shuffled crippled and stiff. Nevertheless, I kept moving, and by the time the sun shot slivers of light through the pine trees, my heels quit hurting.

In an effort to avoid the thick brush near the ridgetop, I traversed side-hill behind Homer's Nose. Now and then I had to cross lesser slopes branching off the main ridge, but for the most part the route required so little effort that I could let my mind drift.

I relived races I had won, or should have won, and others that I hadn't entered because the medals were too small or the shirts too plain or the fees too high. Yet I remembered when the presence of certain spectators had warranted a good effort, well worth those fees.

Those special onlookers invariably waited near the finish line, smiling and giggling and posing, and the tightness of their jeans made it hard for both them and the competitors to run. Bright, multicolored banners flapped and snapped in the wind, and runners staggered or sprinted to the finish. I couldn't help smiling, remembering more—the cherry and swirl of red lips, their softness and pout, their motions and press. I heard whispers, even several moans, but the girls' names escaped me.

Lost in thought, I followed a large ridge that broke to my left and in less than half a mile dropped rapidly in elevation. Soon my mistake was obvious, and I stopped to look about. A climb to regain the better route would require some work, but it wouldn't be dauntingly steep or long. Yet after only a moment's hesitation, I made a choice that I still don't understand. I merely shrugged and kept going down the same way, as if choosing a different route home from school.

Today I tell myself it was youthful wanderlust and a sense of adventure that drove me. The truth is probably simpler, less noble. My choice probably stemmed from my stubborn refusal to accept limits.

As the ground pitched steeper, I worried that it might degenerate into a cliff, but after two hours the slope eased and angled into a meadow where a meandering stream bubbled peacefully. The scenery was so idyllic and I so awestruck that it was easy to imagine I had discovered a hidden paradise, a haven for animals and spirits safely sheltered from the outside world.

I flopped onto my belly and drank from the stream for several minutes, then with water dripping from my chin, rose to my knees to listen. The brook bubbled playfully, quietly, while the wind whispered in the nearby pines. I nodded and even laughed a little, certain the sounds were for me, only me.

Falling

After a few minutes, I moved ahead again, this time with a gradual grade and a constant supply of water. As I walked, I fantasized about luscious young women who, inspired by my presence, sprawled about and sighed like sex-starved debutantes. At any minute I expected to feel the smoothness of blacktop under my boots or hear a car engine's whine. Yet hour after hour nothing broke the calm of the scene, and I quickened my pace at the thought of another hungry night outdoors.

Just as I began to trot, the topography betrayed me. The by now familiar brook tumbled off a breathtaking drop, its spray plunging into a deep chasm toward the distant roar of a larger stream. To my far right, the mountain gave way to a perpendicular precipice, a deeply cut ravine. Ahead of me lay a similar gorge, craggy and dangerous, and far across the expanse two canyons away, a faint zigzag of road beckoned like the finishing tape of a race.

For several minutes I simply stared, trying to come up with a strategy, a plan both prudent and possible, but in the midday stillness, no trails appeared and no helicopter blades chopped at the air. The ease of the previous hours, the enchantment, and the thrill of new country fell away in the face of the challenge before me, and only the sight of the road gave me hope.

Without it, I might have folded or, at least, resigned myself to another night, but now the goal line was visible, reachable. Furthermore, my anger was building until before long I felt the full force of the mountain's betrayal. Homer's Nose had broken its nurturing, loving, easy-walking promise.

"Fuck me." I whispered the words, then raised my head and screamed down the canyon, "FUCK YOU."

The only possible path lay to my right where a collection of half-buried boulders and misshapen trees fought a steep but less-than-vertical grade. I surveyed my inevitable route, then looked away to the faint line of road in the distance. I nodded. It had to be.

I took a few steps into the gorge. My boots slid, freeing rocks and clods of dirt that raced ahead of me. When the grade grew steeper, I turned to face the cliff, grabbing at roots, rocks, and bushes, anything to help me fight gravity's pull.

Then the ground became rockier, tougher to gain a foothold. I clung to a small bush and stared downward to a point fifty feet below me where the mountain became an overhang of smooth stone. I edged to my left, but when my left boot landed on a mossy rock, I slid away, instantly out of control. I grappled desperately for rocks, dirt, anything to arrest my slide but managed only to peel the skin from my fingers. In a panic, I clawed even harder, yet my efforts were no match for gravity, and dirt, dust, and dried leaves whirled out of my hands like ashes in a strong wind.

At the moment that my mouth was gaping for a silent scream, I slid over a mound of roots and rocks that slowed me a little. When my hands passed over something firm, I seized it, straining and grunting, and managed to stop myself, even as debris showered about me for several more seconds.

A spray of blood splashed onto the root I had in my clutch, and when I snorted to clear my nostrils, I felt wetness hit my chest. Another downward glance revealed a rock outcropping above still another airy drop. Desperate, I turned to my other side where a six-foot scrub pine twisted from the cliff, and cautiously, I let go of my life-preserver root to sidle to my left, grabbing again at rocks, plants, and half-buried sticks. At last I reached the little tree, laid hold of its trunk, and exhaled in relief.

Safe for the moment, I coughed at the taste of blood and looked at my shirtfront to see it decorated with bright-red blobs. I couldn't let go to pinch my nose, so instead I closed my eyes and did my best to slow my breathing. Gradually other sounds seemed to return as I hung there for several minutes and listened to a watery roar from far below.

My nosebleed had slowed to a drip when I swung myself down to a rock that offered fair handholds. Somewhere below me a torrent thundered, and as I edged my way down, the din became louder and louder until the noise overtook all other thoughts.

Soon I was close to the rush and roar. I could see a pool beneath a waterfall, but foam played on its surface for only seconds before plummeting over the next drop. With no handholds, I couldn't go upstream, so the downstream route was my only option. I grabbed at bushes to steady myself and followed the water to the next pool, but it was also deep and turbulent, degenerating into a fierce cascade that forced me to continue downstream.

At a chest-high rock covered with pine needles and loose soil, I dug my elbows into the mound hoping to hoist myself up when a sudden acrid smell pulled me up short. The surface was alive with ants, a blanket of black and red insects swarming the ground and scurrying up my arms.

Precariously poised, I had no choice but to endure the crawling and biting until I could pull myself onto the rock. Then and only then did I swipe, slap, and brush away the angry swarm, while uttering a stream of curses I could barely hear over the river's roar.

In a moment, I managed to find a perch atop a tall rock eight feet or so above the water. A tangled dam of boulders, logs, and dirt created a deep pool on the side nearest me, a great fishing hole in less perilous times, but on the far side, the water ran swift and waist-deep in a narrow channel before pitching over yet another thirty-foot cliff.

I studied that far-side channel. Were I to wade it and slip, I'd be swept over the falls and killed, tumbling and falling who knows how far before lodging on a rock or a log, or circling endlessly in some unknown eddy. It could be months or even years before my body was found. I scanned further downstream for a better crossing, to no avail. The bank was sheer and tall and offered no handholds. When I looked back to the water on the far side, this time the channel didn't look so swift or deep.

I shed my pack and without further thought flung it as far as I could. I hoped it would reach some dry rocks beyond the pool, but weighed down by the bundled sleeping bag, it plunked into the water. After a quick breath, I leaped from the rock to splash into the pool, managing to kick to the surface despite my waterlogged boots. With a whoop and a grin, I retrieved my pack from the shallows and clambered onto the rocks at the swift channel's verge.

But I couldn't celebrate, not yet. I forced myself to rest and drink. I wasn't in a hurry to die. I studied the water, trying to figure the lay of the bottom. My hair was drying, my body warming, and soon it was time to act.

I flung my pack across the rushing water onto the bank and ventured out into the current. Up close, the water seemed swifter and choppier than it had from above. Please, God, I prayed, don't let me slip. Don't let me slip.

The water whirled around me forming a miniature rapid, but I stood braced and steady, then moved slowly despite my racing heart. The cold torrent had crept over my abdomen when suddenly I felt my left foot sliding. Bile flooded my mouth. Don't slip, don't slip. No, no.

I regained my balance, fighting the current's force and trying to think above the scream in my head. Two more steps, two more steps, damn it. With water splashing against my chest, I leaned forward and kept easing to my left. My boot struck a rock. I stumbled, grabbed at the water for balance, but kept on my feet. A few more steps and the water fell to my thighs. Two more steps and my knees topped the surface. I turned, sloshed across the shallows, and collapsed onto the safety of dry ground.

Then, with a yell, I rolled onto my back and rubbed handfuls of dry sand through my hair, feeling the chafe on my scalp. Still yelling, I stared and continued to stare into the bright blue sky, gaping and blinking, until everything, even the water, became quiet.

I opened my eyes but couldn't remember shutting them. The afternoon sun was still hot and flushed my face. With a grimace, I rolled onto my knees to gaze at the bank where loose dirt and sand marked the way I must go. With that I stood, shouldered my pack, and began to climb. Only once and only briefly did I stop to stare into the gorge and listen to the river, but as I worked, grunting and gasping, cursing and climbing, my thoughts seemed to linger behind me. Finally atop the ridge, I paused to slump against a rock and as a welcome breeze cooled my face, I closed my eyes.

When I roused to rub more sand from my hair and start

Falling

walking again, my steps fell into a comfortable downhill rhythm, making gentle progress between the trees and bushes. In time I realized that another river lay ahead, but its gentle murmurs and trickles troubled me little. When I reached the source of the sound, I found a wide, slow river and waded across without incident.

Knowing that the road was near, I started up the last slope like a runner in his finishing kick, and after climbing over a clump of thick manzanita bushes, I suddenly fell onto the wonderful smoothness of blacktop. Were anyone else present to see and hear me yell "Yeeesss!" they'd have taken me for a wandering wild man, some homeless schizophrenic whose voices drove him to battle bushes and wrestle dirt. Or maybe I was a bear-mauled hiker, desperate and exhausted, struggling to the road in search of help, first-aid for my wounds before speeding me to the hospital in a wail of sirens.

For the moment, I'd done as much as I could. My legs folded in slow motion as I slumped to the ground and my butt hit the pavement. I didn't try to move but just gazed up at the mountains around me, at the trees and bushes and road that curved downward out of sight.

Within a few minutes, a pickup rounded the curve, and after hitchhiking to the town of Three Rivers, I called my parents, bought some junk food, and waited. Several hours passed before my dad finally drove up. I walked over, carrying my boots, and opened the truck's door.

"You are a pain-in-the-butt kid. I can't believe you got lost. You grew up in the damn woods. What were you thinking?"

"I didn't get lost, and I'm glad to see you too, Dad."

"If you didn't get lost, what're you doing here?"

"This is where I came out. I knew I was going off the backside of Homer's, but I saw some incredible country."

"Yeah, yeah, yeah, but you're still a pain in the butt. Where's your car?"

"Up the South Fork."

"You mean you walked from there?"

"Well, not all the way. I hitchhiked down the road."

"What the hell did you do to your feet?"

"I wore some blisters. Big deal."

"Bullshit. Those feet are infected, and it ain't a big deal to you 'cause you won't have to pay the doctor bill."

"Look, I'm tired. I just want to get home."

He pulled out and drove for a bit in silence.

"So did you have to cross a river?"

"Only two."

"Only two? Sometimes I wonder what you got for brains. Did you even have any food left?"

"I didn't take any food."

My dad looked at me once more, sighed, and continued to drive.

In an hour, we were in the South Fork canyon with the sun sinking toward the horizon, turning the draws dim and forlorn. The slow-paced drive and tedium of conversation drained me, replacing surges of adrenaline with the slow flow of everyday worry. Should I concentrate on the 1,500 or the 5,000 meters in track? Do I have the speed for the 1,500? How fast can I go? Do I want to be a star at a small school or challenged at a big one? Which college is best? What's my major? Math? Engineering? English? History? What do I want to do with my life? Who do I want to meet? Will the women be nice? Will their breasts strain against their tight-fitting tops? Will the bulge in my shorts impress them? Will they climb mountains with me? Will they be fun? Funny? Willing?

The questions swirled in my mind as Homer's Nose came into view, its pinnacle still glowing with the last of the sun's rays.

"Stop, Dad! Stop! Will you look at that?"

He stopped.

"I was up there. I was UP THERE, God damn it. Wooo."

"Pretty impressive, I guess." My dad sounded like he could either be proud of me or question my sanity.

Whatever he thought of me, my victory was more than enough. No longer a dead memory, now the climb was a living extension of myself. The peak, the rivers, the mountains, the bushes, the dangers were all left behind, but the experience had changed some part of me, made me new, different, maybe better – a cougar instead of a housecat, a wolf instead of a dog. Anyone who could do what I'd done could certainly run a faster mile, score with the women, and choose any job — not just repetitive, brain-numbing work, but a career that quickened the pulse and brought new knowledge, evoked new experiences.

Sure, in the future I would climb other mountains, rockier ones, more dangerous, more remote. With raw fingers, I'd cling to cracks again, and with sore and scratched arms I'd pull myself to the top of some peak that only I knew. While feeling the high wind on my face, I'd laugh and remember how, long ago, I had pushed myself to the edge, to a place where survival and death sit side-by-side. I would remember that for the first time, I had truly witnessed the sky, felt the earth's powder and scuff, and heard the heartbeat of my own life.

CHAPTER TWO

Cold Nights

It is so pleasant to sit doing nothing – and therefore so
dangerous. Death through
exhaustion is – like death through freezing – a pleasant one.
-- Reinhold Messner, *The Crystal Horizon*

Clint

"Son of a bitch." My sleeping bag wouldn't fit into my
backpack, and with no rope or cords, I tossed the bag back into
my four-wheel drive. It doesn't matter, I thought, it never gets
cold enough in California to even need a bag.

For several months, I'd been living in a small trailer in
Marysville, attending junior college, growing long hair, training
for the upcoming track season, and thoroughly sick of town life
– car horns blaring and people yelling at 2 a.m., the garbage, the
noise. Disheartening, all of it, especially the on-again off-again
moods of my so-called girlfriend, her unexpected late-night
arrivals, her bashful eyes and assertive body, her needs met now
but never later, always searching, seeking something better or
more sophisticated.

Her name was Lisa. She had pouty lips, blond hair, and
a voice that lay on my brain as sticky as cotton candy – sweet,
light, elusive, yet clingy. "I've got several hours free. I know
what we can do." But after tasting her flimsy, wispy sweetness,
the pleasure would dissolve, and I was back to craving
something more. I wasn't satisfied, neither was she.

"You're not right for me," she'd say. "You're not going
anywhere. We're not going anywhere. I feel like you're not
serious. You don't respect me. You don't care about the things I

want." How could I respond to that?

On a particular January weekend in 1985, the cotton-candy voice in my head was so piercing, so insufferable, that I had to lose myself amidst trees and dirt and mountains. So after driving for two hours, first on highway, then asphalt, then dirt, I found myself grinning, breathing crisp mountain air, and feeling freer, lighter than I had in months.

I set off walking rapidly as if headed for a particular goal, looking back at times to remember my path – the old snag, the clearing, the flat rock, a stretch downhill. My mind idled. I just moved and looked, walked, sometimes ran, sometimes stopped to eat, but rarely rested long. Time was irrelevant as the hours raced by, lost in the sound of my relentless footsteps.

The midday sun slipped silently into afternoon with longer shadows and fleeting light. Now and then, I chuckled to myself, but no one cared that I looked like a madman, not here, anyway. Split times on the track, grades, and calculus tests fell far behind, and even that familiar female voice – softly irritable, sullen and sultry – was quiet. All that mattered was ceaseless motion, up and down hills, through bushes and over streams. In time, the air cooled, and with the approach of dusk the setting sun glowed a soft orange.

At a flat place, I stopped to look around, removing my pack as I did so. I scavenged around for wood and within minutes found enough armfuls of dry, light pine to create an impressive pile. Darkness fell faster than seemed possible, but soon my fire blazed high and warm. I settled down beside it, not entirely at ease. Except for the crackling fire, the night was still and unnerving. No birds whistling, no squirrels barking, and the cloud cover blocked the stars and moon to intensify the gloom.

Memories and questions, of subtle and not-so-subtle conflicts, echoed in my mind, then that female voice returned. "Will you ever cut your hair? Do you like living in this trailer? Where will you go after Yuba College? Do you even care about money and nice things?"

I shook my head to banish those echoes. I had everything under control, a warm fire, a good woodpile, a flat place to sleep.

But the dry pine made such a fast, hot fire that it died down much faster than I'd hoped. Before long I had to get to my feet to retrieve more wood for fuel, and as soon as I settled down again, the scenario repeated itself, a disturbing, unwanted replay.

"I don't feel as much anymore. All we ever do is have sex. Do you even love me? You never say it."

There was no escape. I scanned the ground for more wood, but all that remained were bunches of dry grass and thin, twisty shrubs. Frustrated, I stomped out into the night, and when my eyes adjusted to the dark, I spotted a big, partially buried log. It was so big I could barely wrap my arms around it, but with one heave I lifted the crumbly wood with ease.

I carried the log to the fire and tossed it on, then watched the flames surge and dance red-orange against a black-velvet night.

"That feels good, really good. Don't stop. Don't stop. I love it."

I sat staring into the fire and smiled. I recalled her skin's clean smell underneath her Chanel No. 5, remembered the warmth and wiggle of her body beneath my own, the sweet sweat and wet that she always pretended was not entirely hers.

Another twenty minutes saw the fire dwindle, triggering another stumbling search into the darkness where I found only the lightest pine, airy and rotting. I brought it to the fire, but it didn't last – at first flashes of flame, then glowing cinders, then a faint glow.

"I better go, I need a shower, and I'm not showering here. Have you ever thought about an apartment or, at least, a real bed?"

My search for wood continued to widen, increasingly urgent. With every return, the fire was so nearly out that only with great care could I restart it. And even then the joy, the comfort, didn't last.

"Don't you feel a little tacky? Don't you want something more from life?"

It seemed a harpy's pursuit. A new search in a new direction sent me rushing into the blackness once more, only now I was shivering. Over the next four or five hours, I spent less and less time keeping warm by the fire, more time in the dark and the cold, straining to see, hunting for something, anything to burn.

After hiking all day, eating little, and staggering around half the night in the dark, I felt exhausted and my thoughts were fogged. Sleep crept ever closer, stalking. Now I stumbled in the dark, violently shaking and cursing, when something loomed up—a long log, I hoped, not just a deceptive pile of boulders. It had to be a log, just had to.

I took a step forward and fell across it, the feel of wood reviving my spirits. Renewed, I dragged the log toward my fire, and although parts crumbled off here and there, it didn't matter. The biggest catch of the night, it was my best chance to survive until dawn.

The log caught and burned well. I adopted a fetal position on the ground, warm on the fire's side but cold on my back. When thoughts of frostbite teased, I closed my eyes and did my best to reassure myself. You've got it made now. This should last through the night, no problem. Time to sleep.

I awoke with a shiver. The fire had waned, making everything colder, darker. I staggered upright, shaking, to pull more of the log onto the fire and to blow it into flame. Then I lay back down and stared into the firelight, calculating, assuring myself that dawn was near. This log will make it, no problem. Light's just around the corner.

The fire slowly dwindled until just a few coals glowed. I crawled closer, shaking yet wanting to save the log. Within a few minutes, though, I had no choice but to pull more of the log onto the fire. The flames surged and my shakes abated. Gradually, grudgingly, I consigned more and more of the log to the fire until I sacrificed the final piece to restart the flames. In my tired mind, the end of the log meant the end of the night. This should do it. I've made it. Dawn is almost here.

Exhausted, I crashed into a deep sleep, a kaleidoscope of vibrant colors and dancing young women. Their bodies twisted and stretched, rocked and bounced, and the motion became suggestive, then seductive, as lips parted moist and hot breath

began to pant. The culminating kiss tingled with energy but
brought with it a voice both familiar and strident, alluring and
whining, the sound of it distorted, warped like an old vinyl LP,
and far removed from the flicker and smolder of a dying fire.

"Just sleep . . . sleep . . . just sleep."
The lights on the Ferris wheel tilted from vertical to
horizontal, float-falling like bubbles to a white-sand floor,
and after pulsing and dimming once or twice, their radiance
vanished altogether in a stillness that was both dreamy and
unnerving.

"Sleep . . . sleep . . . No . . . no . . . We did it already. Just
sleep."
She rolled over, a smooth back in place of her breasts.
Her bottom rested below the sheets, satin sheets that chilled and
aroused me. I reached for her, my hand slithering lower and
lower, but I couldn't feel her. A strangled yelp escaped me as I
groped wildly, trying to touch a fleshy buttock that wasn't there.

When I opened my eyes, it was too dark to see. My right
arm was extended, my bare hand felt cold and wet. I drew all my
limbs under my body like a dying beetle. My eyes closed.

"Sleep . . . sleep."
Her hand caressed the dashboard, then the knob of the
stereo – fiery-red nails cranking the bass beat, the sync blaring
above, the thump pumping below. Her body moved with the
music, grinding spandex against leather, rocking rhythmically
in her tight, too-short shorts until sweat dewed her skin. Her
blonde hair tossed wildly as her head bobbed to the music, her
mouth open, framed by slick red lips. Now she was panting,
shadow fucking on a contoured, custom seat, and her voice
purred breathily.

"Is this your Corvette? Is it? Is it?"
Without moving, I opened my eyes to look around. The
fire was out. I wiggled forward into the warm ash and closed my
eyes.

"Sleep . . ." But — "Just sleep."
Time was running out, people stirring, handing in their
tests, whispering, exhaling with relief. My heart thumped –

some mistake, some mistake, had to be. I wasn't done. The clock showed 2:55, and I clawed at my test to find the first question.

"Over what range is $F(x)$ infinite?"

That was all, nothing more, no equation. I flipped the page and found it blank.

"Time's up; hand in your tests."

No, hold on, no!

I jolted awake to a dusting of fresh snow and felt wetness on the back of my neck. Yet I didn't feel cold, and I didn't shake. I tried to tense my muscles and move my limbs, vigorously or so I imagined, but in reality I crept as slowly as a cold lizard.

"Fuck you, this is not gonna happen." Still hunkered down, I twisted, undulated, and fought the ground, generating a spray of ash and snowy powder that felt cool as it settled on my head.

"I . . . WILL . . . NOT . . . DIE!" I thrashed the ground again, humping and straining, burrowing my head into the remains of the fire. After many minutes of work, I rested, panting and blinking in the blackness. That was when the shakes started again, mild and at first only involving my chest, but the shivers grew stronger and spread to my back, thighs, and arms. Soon my entire body convulsed and contorted.

Even though the next several hours saw me cursing, shaking, and wallowing in grime, in my mind the outcome was no longer in doubt. By the time the first slash of sunshine hit the mountainside, I was already walking, warming.

The day before, I had lost myself in the hike, escaping the rush and worry of modern life. Now the trek back focused me like the final lap of a race, preparing me for the finishing tape as well as the cooler-than-not shower. By evening, the finish line was near and the hike was over.

I stood in a phone booth, dusty coins in hand, staring at my four-wheel drive atop a tow truck. An International Scout, the model was so old it was no longer manufactured, and years before with some cheap paint and thirty minutes of creative zeal, I'd rendered it in camouflage. No beauty, its upholstery was torn, the internal padding bulging and splaying like the entrails of a gutted buck. The AM radio still worked, but only if reception was good. While the camouflage remained, now the freezing night had busted its water pump. Poor old Scout. Then I remembered the coins in my hand. I exhaled, slotted in the coins, and dialed.

"Hello."

"Lisa, it's me." My tongue felt thick.

"Clint, did you hear about the new restaurant in Sacramento, Antoinette's? It's supposed to be really elegant – real china, cloth napkins, a maître d', everything."

"Lisa, we need to talk."

"That's what we're doing. Anyway, this place — "

"Lisa, listen to me. I'm not what you want in a guy, and to be perfectly honest, I don't think — "

"What are you saying? You ass, are you breaking up, breaking up with me?"

"Yeah, I'm breaking up with you. It's time. I'm sorry."

But I wasn't sorry, and a few months later, I moved away and met Ursula, a girl from the other side of the world, a creature with cocoa skin, the voice of a princess, and kisses that tasted of sweet mango.

CHAPTER THREE

Creature

Wait a minute, baby,
Stay with me a while.
Said you'd give me light,
But you never told me about the fire.
-- from Fleetwood Mac's "Sara"

Ursula

The first time I saw Clint, sex was not foremost on my mind. I was on holiday from Durban, South Africa, visiting my sister, Beverly, in Porterville, California. I happened to glance out the window when a camouflaged, Army-appearing van stopped across the street and a man with long scraggly hair stepped out. He had on blue-and-white-striped running tights, an orange sweatshirt, and ghastly green shoes.

"What in the world is that?" I stared and blinked, speaking to myself, but Beverly answered.

"Oh, that's Clint. He runs cross-country with Thevi and lives across the street. He's a nice chap, you'll meet him later. We're invited to dinner."

At dinner, this skinny, fashion-challenged *rondlooper* – I'd have called him then; now I'd say hippie – conversed with me and inquired nonstop about South Africa. We started with politics, apartheid, and the effects of economic sanctions, then we discussed Table Mountain, Durban's weather, and juicy mangoes. I remember his hair tossed in every conceivable direction, he often spoke while attempting to eat, and he dressed like a color-blind derelict. But his eyes were clear, wet-blue and steady, and as he looked at me, I remembered Durban's beautiful, warm ocean. I simply had to smile.

A week later, Beverly and her family moved to Fresno, where I was to join them in another week's time. So Beverly arranged for Clint to fetch me, and soon I found myself riding in that same rickety-rattling, army-looking van with a long-haired semi-stranger who questioned me endlessly about the school system in South Africa.

"Did you like high school? What subjects did you take? Did you graduate? How many years did you go? What did you do after high school? How many years did you go to Technikon? At what age do you start school in South Africa?"

He asked nonstop questions, and I continued to answer, adding personal stories and what I hoped were insightful anecdotes. I simply assumed he was curious about our school system. But Clint had an ulterior motive. He wanted to ask me on a date but was afraid I might only be about fourteen years old. Instead of simply asking my age, he went through this elaborate inquiry. About the time we reached Fresno, he must have concluded that I was of age.

He first became quiet, then casually asked as if asking about my favorite ice cream, "Would you like to go with me to see Aerosmith next week? You know, somehow I've got two tickets." He was so silly, delightful really. He made it seem he had accidentally bought two tickets, and one would go to waste if I said no. Even though Aerosmith wasn't an orchestra I recognized, I agreed to go, wondering if they might be a jazz band.

In South Africa, a concert is typically a sophisticated and relaxing experience. You dress in your finest, you go, you sit, you listen, and you leave, and then you discuss the performance, while sipping from a glass of Riesling or a cup of Five Roses tea. I soon learned about rock concerts in America — the attire or lack thereof, the crowds, the pushing, the smoke, and above all the noise.

Clint took me to Fresno's Selland Arena and led me onto the floor area near the stage. With the lights still on, hundreds of concertgoers milled about, smoking, chatting, laughing. At the same time, the head-high speakers played popular tunes that could scarcely be heard over the countless conversations and isolated chants of "Aer-o-smith!"

I was trying to fathom it all when Clint leaned toward me and murmured, "When Aerosmith comes on, there'll be a big push toward the stage. You have to stay close and hold your position." Now I understand, but at the time, he might as well have been speaking Swahili.

When the lights dimmed, everyone ran toward the stage, pushing, grasping, and screaming. Someone grabbed my shoulder, pulling me backward, and a score of people shoved by me. As the first song began and laser lights cut across the stage, I was squeezed tightly in the crush and simply could not breathe. When the pressure eased, I sought Clint in the crowd but couldn't find him.

A man to my right, with a scraggly beard and long hair, tottered back and forth shouting, "Don't fight it, don't fight it, bring on the tits!"

I was more than a little relieved to spy Clint weaving through the crowd to arrive at my side. He smiled reassuringly.

"Ursula, what happened?"

"They pushed me." I didn't know what else to say.

In all the mad frenzy, I couldn't see the stage. A couple of blondes, sitting on their guys' shoulders, undulated as if possessed or drunk or both. With my urging, we retreated from the floor to climb some stairs and find some seats. It seemed utterly mad, choosing to be on the floor amidst that throng. But Clint began sighing, looking about and fidgeting. Did he miss being one with that crowd, closer to one of those wild, boozed-up blondes?

But when Clint regained his focus, it was worse. Only rarely did he glance my way or smile, and he never tried to hold my hand. He simply sat there, staring, mouth ajar, until I felt as if I'd come to my first American concert with a statue.

After the concert, Clint did manage to rejoin the living and drove me to Bev's apartment.

"Would you mind if I walked you to the door and kissed

you goodnight?"

What now? I felt uneasy being so far from home and in company with a long-haired almost-stranger. In addition, I hadn't known what to make of the concert or Clint's behavior there. I answered as well as I knew how.

"You may walk me to the door, but I don't know about kissing me goodnight."

After that, Clint and I dated every couple of weeks, but he never tried to kiss me or even hold my hand. When we sat together in the shade at Murray Park or tucked away in some dark movie theater, I thought he might become more amorous, and if he did, I often wondered what I'd do. Slap him? Push him away? Withdraw and act shocked? Or might his touch be too much for me? Might I, in the darkness, let my lips part a bit and press forward? I certainly knew of the risks.

In South Africa, some guys had been insistent. I was a waif, eighty-four pounds, so I had to be cautious in dealing with men. I had been eighteen when, alone with a reputable young teacher named Lennie, he pinned me on the living-room carpet on the pretense of demonstrating a karate move. I was stuck and struggling, not panicked, but well aware that I might soon be embroiled in a lot more than karate. I remember thinking I should be able to break free, but he was stronger than I thought, and as I twisted and strained, I saw something in his hand — a red-wrapped packet marked "Trojans – Lubricated Latex Condom."

At that, I went mad. Surprised, Lennie released me, and I sprang up fuming.

"You bloody leave!" I yelled, and he did, but I continued to seethe even after slamming the door. After a bit I felt my body relax, but even after locking the door, my hands still trembled, and when I tried to walk, my legs felt like rubber bands.

I felt like crying, but I did not. I simply took a deep breath, straightened my skirt, and told myself that I would not dwell on it. It was done. He had left. I was fine. I was home, story finished.

But in the States, everything seemed different, intimidating. People spoke bluntly, directly, even in public. The men watched rugby on television, called it "football," and didn't seem to be bothered that most of the athletes were Black. The women had attitudes, careers, or both, and the television was full of violence and sex, although everyone pretended otherwise. My sister Beverly and her husband Thevi were here, but my other sisters, my brother, and most importantly, my parents were in faraway South Africa. With an abundance of time and freedom, I was compelled to make careful choices.

To my gratitude and his credit, Clint never rushed me, despite opportunities, and I felt comfortable becoming friends. We conversed for hours, on splintery park benches, on the telephone, at track meets, and in restaurants, laughing, telling stories, and sometimes eating greasy chow mein.

As we spent more and more time together and became better friends, he confided in me about his diagnosis of multiple sclerosis. I couldn't see that it made any difference in his life, as he seemed to have no trouble with physical activities, and his brain was certainly as active as ever.

One day in a Safeway, I introduced Clint to mangoes. I bought a nice ripe one, and once back inside his camouflaged car, instructed him on the "best" way to eat it. With a straight face, I told him peeling a mango was far and away the best method. He never suspected a thing. In short order, he was peeling the fruit and rolling it around in his increasingly sticky fingers. With the mango dripping all over the place, I said, "Dive in." He did, smearing juice all over his face and arms. It made such a mess that he had to open the car door to let mango juice splatter onto the parking lot.

By the time the mango was eaten and the juice shower done, I was laughing so I could barely offer Clint a tissue. A good sport in spite of being the brunt, before heading for the washroom, he just smiled and wagged his finger at me.

But that was and is Clint—no common sense. He wore basketball shoes in the rain, scattered rubbish in his car, dined from paper plates, and seemed to purposefully ignore practical matters such as finances. His arrogant belief that he could do anything irritated me, and he acted as if good grades were his birthright. Yet at other times, I found his lack of pretense disarming, endearing really.

His attitude toward other people impressed me as well. We were in a grocery store stocking up for a picnic when a scruffy woman with bare, dirty feet came along. Her hair was long, uncombed, and hung partly over her face. Her unrestrained breasts fell to her belly. Thinking she was homeless and on drugs, I was veering away from her when she happened to spot Clint. At first, her mouth hung open, and she merely stared, but then she shouted "Clint!" and rushed forward to throw her arms around him.

Clint merely chuckled and returned her embrace before turning to introduce me.

"Sally, this is Ursula. Ursula, Sally and I went to high school together."

As they chatted to catch up, I learned a few things and deduced more. Sally had become pregnant in high school and dropped out, then eight months ago had borne a second child. She and the children were living in a trailer with an older, rather demanding man.

As Sally recounted these details her hair fell back to reveal a terrible purplish swelling around her left eye. Seeing it, Clint blurted out, "Jesus, what happened to you?"

"Oh, one of those things that happen, you know. Frank didn't mean it. He's usually sweet, but if he has too much to drink, well —"

She waved her hand as if shooing away a fly, then went on. "Besides, that day I was being a real bitch. I called the police, so it's all good now. But you know, you two look so happy, you make a wonderful couple."

We weren't really a couple yet, certainly not a let's-drink-some-shots-and-pummel-each-other couple, but I was not in the mood to explain. We simply smiled and said "Thank you" and "Nice to see you" and "Stay in touch."

Later when we were in the Scout, I asked Clint about her, expecting him to downplay their association with "I barely knew her," or "That's one crazy woman." I thought he'd laugh at her black eye and filthy feet, but he never did. He smiled and shook his head, but he refused to belittle her. Instead, he told me

Falling

what he knew of her life, in a distinctly sad tone.

One of six kids whose disabled mother struggled to hold the family together, Sally had known Clint since the seventh grade, when she loved school and wrote poetry. But by high school she'd gained a reputation for being wild and using drugs. She and Clint were just casual friends until their senior year when Sally broke up with her boyfriend and asked Clint for a date. Their resulting fling was intense but lasted only a couple of days. They parted on good terms, Clint to go to college and Sally to go back to her boyfriend.

After telling me this, Clint shook his head and sighed, his blue eyes mesmerizing and steady.

"When you look at Sally, you see a dirty woman hooked on drugs and in an abusive relationship. That's how she is now. But when I look at her, I still see the bubbly girl who wrote poetry too sad and deep for her years. I see the feisty youngster who loved to dance and laugh and speak her mind. She was never a cheerleader. She never sought to fit in or to gain approval. Her smile was flirty but not fake. She was real and intelligent, but she just made terrible choices."

I could have kissed him. The moment was so quiet and tender that I couldn't move. I just stared and stared. When Clint tilted his head toward me and leaned closer, I couldn't move, couldn't respond. And so the moment passed.

Two weeks later, it was Easter, and I was staying with Beverly in Fresno, while Clint was eighty miles away in Porterville. I'd begun to think Clint might have tired of me and was pursuing some unknown but willing girl who knew nothing of mangoes and Africa.

Then Bev's doorbell rang and there was Clint, grinning and trying to seem casual.

"You know, I was planning this road trip to Northern Cal to visit friends, and my friend Robert was supposed to go, but he decided not to at the last minute. It's a long drive if you don't have anyone to talk to, and I thought you might want to see the country. So would you want to take a trip with me?"

I was reluctant until Bev encouraged me. "Come on, Ursh. Go have fun. It'll be great. You can do it." So by and by, I agreed to go.

It was a long drive. Clint and I talked about everything under the sun, yet still impersonally, as if our near-miss, close-enough-to-kiss moment had never happened.

Soon we were in Marysville nearing Doug's house. One of Clint's friends from college, Doug still lived with his parents, who were the most gracious of hosts and served us a delectable sparerib dinner with baby potatoes. I ate so much that I had to decline dessert.

Everyone seemed enthralled with the exotic foreigner and asked countless questions about South Africa, apartheid, my views on economic sanctions, and my impressions of the States. When bedtime came, I didn't know what to expect until Doug showed us to a guest bedroom with twin beds.

I went into the bathroom to get ready for bed and put on my pajamas. Then while Clint was in the bathroom, I snuggled into my little bed, smiling to myself. I was certainly surprised when he emerged from the bathroom, wearing light-blue briefs that pictured an ice cream sundae complete with hot fudge, walnuts, and a rather prominent banana. "Have A Treat," was the legend under it, the goofiest thing I had ever seen. I started to laugh and pulled my covers closer in mock fear.

Clint was laughing too, looking down as if seeing his attire for the first time. Soon we were laughing so hard that Clint collapsed onto the floor with a thud. I couldn't stop laughing even as I asked whether he was hurt. Finally he staggered to his feet, wiping his eyes. "Okay, okay," he said, "no dessert for you. And no more laughing at my banana."

That set me off anew. He was so hilarious, so completely silly.

"Goodnight, then, you silly Creature," he said, still laughing, and hopped into his bed as I reached to dim the light. Before falling asleep, I managed only to say goodnight and smile to myself under the covers.

The next morning as Clint gave me a tour of Marysville, including Yuba College and a city park, we strolled along talking and, in time, holding hands. It felt natural, perfectly innocent.

The sun was shining in the park, ducks quacking on

the pond, and we walked cheery as schoolchildren, swinging
our arms, our fingers intertwined. Clint told me how happy
he was that I had agreed to come with him on this trip. Then
he shifted to a more serious subject—his obsession with
competitive running and his disappointment in his recent track
performances. I saw that it bothered him. Although I already
knew he had multiple sclerosis, I didn't see how it could be
to blame as he was strolling with me, speaking smoothly and
effortlessly.

I told him more about myself, even the incident with
Lennie. He listened without comment, then simply squeezed my
hand.

After several pleasant hours, we started on the road to
Eureka, and once again we revealed to one another more of our
stories, our lives. In Eureka, however, our fortunes changed, as
Clint could not reach any of his former cross-country teammates.

Apparently, all his friends either had moved or had
unlisted numbers, for he didn't reach a one. It was dark by then,
and we sat in the Scout in the rain, counting our money, and
wondering how to get a hotel room with only fourteen dollars
and a Texaco credit card.

It seemed comical to me, but Clint tormented himself
searching for a solution. At last I stopped him mid-sentence.
"What would you do," I asked, "if you were here alone?"

Surprised, he said at once, "I'd buy some food at a gas
station, put it on the card, and just drive down to the redwoods
and spend the night in the Scout."

I smiled. "Then let's go."

Relieved, he revved up the Scout.

The local Texaco mini-mart's stock was a revelation to
me—nuts and health drinks, donuts and sodas. I wasn't actually
hungry, but not knowing what lay ahead, I thought we should
take along adequate nourishment. In the end, I bought just one
thing for myself, a bottle of chocolate milk.

The hour was late, and it was still drizzling when we
rolled into Rockefeller Forest south of Eureka. Clint drove along
a splashy dirt road to park at a flat place near a trailhead. It
wasn't a campsite, no toilet facilities or other cars, just countless

trees and a rain so quiet that I wanted to whisper.

Clint reached and turned on the dim overhead light as we took stock of our mini-mart score – mango nectar for Clint, and chocolate milk for me. Mine tasted processed, artificial, and I returned it to the brown paper sack before turning toward Clint. He guzzled half his drink and smiled.

"Is it good?" I don't know why I asked, but Clint nodded and handed me the can.

The drink was sweet, almost too sweet, and surprisingly potent, as if it needed additional water. It made me think of Durban and its rich sea air, its street vendors with their ripe, swollen mangoes and pink-fleshy guavas. I thought of the people haggling, chatting, and working, always trying for a bit more, something sweeter, juicier, something enticing and untried. I smiled, handing the can back to Clint with a "thank you."

Clint drank the remainder without pause and tossed the can to the far-back of the Scout, but then his words troubled me, as I was not thinking of sleep. "I'll let you have the back since it's a little roomier, and I'll take the front. It's likely to get cold in here, but, don't worry, I'll start the car and run the heater every so often."

"Don't you want to sit up and chat a bit?" My question instantly made my heart race, and my grip tightened on my brown paper sack.

After a pause, Clint shifted and straightened, turning his body to look directly at me. "It's probably obvious, but I always want to chat with you." His eyes were steady on me for several moments, quiet, uncomfortable moments. I tried to speak, but my mind seemed to be screaming something incoherent, and I could not seem to breathe or to move, except to clutch my sack tighter.

Without looking away, Clint reached down and covered my hand with his own. His fingers waited for a time before squeezing my hand. My grip relaxed a bit.

But I simply could not let go of the sack. I wanted to, but for the life of me, I simply could not, and the tension from my hand seemed to swell into my throat, making my voice croak.

Falling

"Help me, help me."

Then Clint kissed me, lightly and swiftly at first, but gradually longer, deeper, until my tongue flickered and ached with the taste of mango. And he touched me, a testing contact at first, but then more and more bold, until fondling, exploring, and finding places I hardly knew I had.

My mind continued to scream, but I was moving now, feeling and breathing, and I dropped my paper sack. Clint felt warm and strong and safe, but on this occasion, I knew he was quite wrong, at least, with regard to his weather forecasting. The night never would turn cold for it tasted like home, and at certain times, Durban can become rather hot.

CHAPTER FOUR

Nuptials

Ursula

After our night amid the redwoods, Clint and I became inseparable. Although on occasion I did express my desire to return to South Africa, admittedly I was conflicted, and my life and plans slowly became rooted in the States.

It was a hot June day, and Clint and I were driving to his parents' house up a mountain called Blue Ridge. The stifling air made it difficult for me to breathe, so when Clint wanted to stop for a swim in Bear Creek, I offered little resistance.

"Mightn't we be late?"

Clint smiled. "I don't think they'll start without us. Besides, you're a sexy Creature in your birthday suit."

"Don't you wish! I have my bathing suit with me, and we definitely have no time for silliness."

The water felt wonderful, even though I only waded. As for Clint, he swam, jumped from a tall rock into a pool, and caught a baby snake that I insisted he keep far from me.

We got back in the Scout for the rest of the ride, and the road dust collected on our damp skin and clothes, making us less than presentable when we arrived at the summit of Blue Ridge.

Clint's father greeted us smiling. "Hey, the bride and groom are finally here. Everyone else is here. You two better hustle and get ready."

Yes, we were going to be married. My parents couldn't be with us, but my mother made me a truly gorgeous white gown and sent it to me from South Africa. I showered quickly and put it on, thinking of her love and care.

Yet others of my family were able to attend: my sister, her husband, my uncle and aunt, a niece, and several cousins. On Clint's side, his immediate family as well as both sets of grandparents, aunts, uncles, and more cousins joined us.

A family friend, a Native American shaman named Lalo, presided over the ceremony, making our nuptials a mixture of Native American, East Indian, and African. While it was not something I'd spent years anticipating and planning, it was splendid even so.

Later that night, after Clint fell asleep, I lay awake thinking how different we two were. I had absolutely no desire to climb mountains or to make myself suffer in some silly way. Why had Clint wanted me, chosen me above all others? Was it something inherent in my person, something special, or was it simply the heat between my thighs?

Clint

Ursula helped me to see that there was more to life than endless competition. After we married, I quit running and accepted, to some extent, that I had multiple sclerosis (MS), a poorly understood illness that destroyed nerve conduction and led to an erratic, yet often progressive, course of disability. In MS the fatty sheaths around nerves are destroyed. These myelin sheaths allow for nerve conduction, but if disrupted, simple movements become clumsy or impossible.

At the time there were no bona fide treatments for MS, except prednisone was frequently given for short periods during an exacerbation. Even if treatment for MS had been available and I'd wanted it, the point was moot, for my pre-existing condition ruled out health insurance for me.

In truth, at that point I didn't need treatment. I could ride a bicycle, play basketball, and climb mountains all day long. At most, I might begin to limp if I overdid it or got overheated. Like many MS patients, I had trouble with heat or fever, but what was of greater importance for me was being happily married. My new wife was my best friend, and I could still handle her heat — most of the time.

CHAPTER FIVE

Frills and Monsters

Ursula

I suspect Clint goes into the wilds simply to test himself, to see how he will respond when in danger and free of society's constraints. Unfortunately, with those constraints gone, it's easy to become rather crude, as Clint can often be.

But I shouldn't be surprised. Clint's entire family swears freely at the dinner table and spreads "shit" and "goddamn" on their conversations like condiments at a picnic. Rifles and pistols and knives lie scattered throughout the house as casually as potted plants.

We hadn't been dating long when I opened their refrigerator to confront the enormous, uncovered, hindquarter of a deer. With hoof still attached, it was dripping blood onto the vegetable crisper. Stunned, I spoke to Clint about it, but he simply shrugged as if his parents had forgotten to tidy their bed.

Back home in South Africa, I'd come from a less than affluent, far from above-it-all home myself. My father worked as an auto mechanic, while my mother raised five girls and one boy. My mother ran a tight ship; she simply had to. Under apartheid, we in the Indian community could not afford nonsense or recklessness, for we'd witnessed the arrests of schoolchildren and heard terrifying whispered stories of beatings and chokings and even electric shocks.

So we were brought up to attend school, mind our affairs, and resign ourselves to daily indignities – white shopkeepers' suspicious glares, whites-only beaches and toilets, and the pervasive yet ever surprising force that made waitresses, clerks, and cashiers turn away in mid-sentence to assist fairer-skinned customers.

Despite many years of dedicated service, my father was never promoted. Yet he trained several chaps who rapidly advanced to head mechanic, thanks to their vanilla skin or Boer heritage. He knew that objections too strident or bold were dangerous and generated walking papers or worse.

And even minor transgressions, crimes easily forgiven in the Indian community, brought profound consequences in the South African courts. The judges in their curly white wigs might appear humorous and harmless, but their sentences could be utterly venomous. My brother was twenty years old when he committed his first breach of the law. He forged a check for 48 Rand, about 20 American dollars, and was sentenced to two years in Cape Town's infamous Pollsmoore Prison. And in South Africa at that time, because nonwhite criminals were not entitled to probation, my brother served his entire sentence.

Just once, my mother rode a bus for twelve hours to have a twenty-minute visit with him, the two of them separated by a twenty-meter space. She never elaborated about it except to say that her visit was rather short. Finances prevented further trips.

But the country around Durban was extraordinarily beautiful, lush and warm, with blue skies, soft beaches, and the most succulent fruit. The air had a richness beyond measure, a strange moist, sweet smell that made one want to laugh or feast or dance. This champagne air made it easy to trade smiles with boys, even if they were over-eager or not very handsome. In Durban, it was easy to giggle over secrets with a friend and for a short while forget about work and school, even forget apartheid.

And beyond the law, families had other serious concerns. Without exception, my older sisters fell pregnant at young ages, one by one, to be sentenced to marriages that were not necessarily good and loving.

Often Clint wishes me to behave in ways I find indiscreet or even sleazy, while my nature is more reserved. After our marriage, while my parents were visiting, staying with us in a studio apartment, Clint would kiss me and squeeze me and pat my bum as if my parents were nowhere about. It drove me mad, and each time he touched me while they were there, I'd hark back to that obscene deer leg in his mother's refrigerator. But there was no way to change him. He simply refused to see.

He addressed my parents by their first names and talked to them as if they were his high-school chums, and "yes sir" and "yes ma'am" were not a part of his vocabulary. He would tell my parents risqué jokes with no hesitation, not even the slightest blush.

"Hey, Veda, did you hear the one about the ugly guy who wanted to get laid?"

My poor mother would listen to his joke and laugh, but she was only being courteous. Such behavior was not part of her social code.

Thinking it would be a treat for them, Clint decided we should all go camping together, and he brought along a mattress for them, tied atop the Scout. At the campsite my parents did well for city dwellers, fishing and taking in the sights, enjoying the fresh air and water, exploring, venturing a short way outside of camp. And when night arrived, the four of us settled about the campfire for sleep – my parents on the mattress, Clint and I in a double sleeping bag on the ground.

Then during the night my father roused us to report that someone or something was making noise and rolling rocks by the stream. Clint propped up on one elbow and listened briefly.

"It's all right," he said. "Just wake me up again if something licks you on the face."

In South African city people, his joking words evoked sirens, shouts, and gunfire. After that my mother hid under the covers but could not sleep. My father arose and sat hunched over by the fire, shivering, stoking the coals, and staring into the blackness on full alert. All night he sat quiet and watchful, looking into the darkness, on guard against some mysterious beast.

I nudged Clint and whispered for him to bloody well do something, but he didn't stir. After my third attempt, he whispered, "I love you. Go to sleep, Creature."

I should have been upset, but for the life of me, I could not decide upon the proper course of action – awaken, relocate, shout, start the car, shoot the rifle? All of a sudden, my fears seemed comical, as if bears were hiding under the car or monsters behind the trees. I grinned and had to giggle. I couldn't help it.

In a matter of moments, I simply could not keep my eyes open. I began to drift back to sleep, remembering our home at Mobeni Heights, feeling the sting of red curry spice on my tongue, and smelling Durban's sweet ocean air. But before falling truly asleep, I smiled once more, and as I drifted off, I found myself holding one of Clint's hands close to my chest.

CHAPTER SIX

Buttons

Ursula

At times, Clint fails to appreciate the effect on others of his exuberance and folly. In college, for example, he managed to graduate and to complete a teaching certificate, but then, seemingly on a whim, decided to pursue a career in medicine. We were living on a meager income, yet he remained completely indifferent to our poverty.

While Clint's a plucky sod for whom I generally have considerable admiration, he leaves all the finances in my hands and expects me to perform miracles. In contrast, many Indian men in South Africa maintain strict control of their money, treat their wives like children, and dole out a monthly allowance. I don't advocate such an approach, but when the bills are due and our accounts overdrawn, I can't help feeling a tinge of envy.

Even before medical school, it was all we could do to stay afloat. At one point I was unable to pay the bill for Clint's textbooks – $ 512.98 – and had to carry a significant balance on the MasterCard. If I had bothered to tell Clint, he would have taken little interest, just taken more courses and bought even more books the next term.

During college he worked the night shift at a gas station but didn't find that enough of a challenge. So on one occasion, he registered for thirty units, all of them quite difficult courses, then studied thereafter as if possessed. Forget eating and sleeping and conversing with me. For months, his entire life was devoted to studying, drinking coffee, and asking me to decrease the volume on the television, in between attempts to seduce me.

Falling

There was never any foreplay or slow kiss, no time for such pleasantries. At times, I was resentful and sent him back to his books. At other times, I was so lonely and far from home, bored and tired of Mr. Letterman, that I helped him with the buttons.

Even early in our marriage, Clint despised buttons, fumbled and struggled with them terribly, and in hindsight his MS was probably affecting his dexterity. But I am fond of buttons myself, as I am with regard to sewing stylish clothes. Buttons are an essential part. They are simple and efficient and tasteful, and I am able to open tiny pins and repair four-eyed fasteners rapidly, easily, without becoming bothered or creating a fuss. The only time I do have difficulty, tug and lose patience, is when I am nervous or rushing for some reason or another.

Anyway, while Clint was grappling with thirty units, he typically rode the bus in a rare effort to save money, except that on one particular day he drove the Scout instead. Mister I-Don't-Need-Sleep finished his classes and caught the bus back home.

The next morning he was frantic.

"Where's the Scout? It's gone. Oh, my God, somebody stole it!"

I should have known nobody in his or her right mind would steal a camouflaged Scout, but Clint assured me that every hooligan everywhere wanted it because it had four-wheel drive. Our neighbor at the apartment complex further bolstered Clint's delusion, saying he was "absolutely certain" the Scout had been parked outside the night before. So we called the police, reported the theft, and waited.

Later that same day, I was riding the bus myself, complaining to my bus-driver friend Rebecca that my back hurt, my shoes pinched, and I felt like screaming or crying or both. I bemoaned being far from home, tired, hot and hurting, and disgusted that anyone would steal our old vehicle.

Rebecca said, "You mean that camouflaged Jeep-looking thing I always see at Cal State?"

"Yes, and it was our only car. I can't see why anyone would steal it."

Rebecca blinked. "Well, I just saw your Jeep parked at

Cal State a while ago." Immediately everything became clear.

I called Clint and then the police, explaining that our car had not actually been stolen by a band of demented car thieves but merely misplaced.

"Lady," the officer said, "I'm not sure I follow you, but we'll send somebody out."

After Clint finished work and we went to retrieve his beloved Scout, he stood next to it, hands in his pockets, smiling like a proud father. To me, he looked just wonderful, like a straight-laced all-American high school kid about to go to his first dance. When I asked him who found his wayward auto, he grinned guiltily and wrote my name on the Scout's dusty back window.

A few minutes later, while we were inside our flat and continuing to be affectionate but shy, a female officer arrived to sort out the case of the "misplaced car." She was young, looked a tad anxious and stiff in her uniform, and held her pen tightly as she took notes. But as the story unfolded, her smile began to match my own.

The room was pleasant, and the open patio door carried a nice breeze as night approached, but as I spoke to the policewoman, the breeze dwindled and our flat started to become uncomfortably warm. I told of and laughed at Clint's madness of enrolling in so many units, his single-minded silliness, and his hilarious certainty that his precious Scout had been kidnapped.

Clint beamed the entire time, his face frequently flushed with laughter. He fanned himself with his hand, and although he seemed to want to interrupt me, he satisfied himself with squeezing my hand under the table.

I could not be stopped, not on this night; I was far and away too heated, especially after all the studying and seriousness of the past weeks, months – the spilled coffee, the cold sheets, the quiet. By the time I was finished, convulsions of laughter were as common as words, and I could hardly breathe.

I tried in vain to cool my body by jiggling the front of my blouse. Then I attempted to unfasten my shirt's top button, but my fingers shuddered so awkwardly that it took a considerable amount of time.

In due course we all settled down. Clint shook his head, smiling, and the policewoman closed her notebook, wiped her eyes, and stood.

Her exit should have ushered in cool air, but the night was extraordinarily warm, and as Clint said "goodbye" and closed the door, my fingers were already trembling and tugging on those bloody buttons.

CHAPTER SEVEN

Medical School Secrets

Clint

"I miss the squawking and strut—" A coughing fit broke up her voice, and as the woman covered her mouth with her hand and shut her eyes, her flabby body shuddered beneath her faded hospital gown. After the paroxysm passed, her eyes fluttered open, and she raised her weary, black-coffee face, dabbing at her lips with a tissue.

"You lost me, Sharon." I offered a wastebasket for her used tissue and then waited as another round of coughing began.

When the hacking eventually stopped, Sharon spat into her tissue and frowned at the rust-colored smear before saying, "Junior's dead."

"Your cockatoo? What happened?"

"Baseball players, rock-throwers, ain't nothing new, dumb high-school kids is all." She coughed on the words then gagged, almost vomited, and even after managing to swallow, her mouth remained agape.

"They killed him, pulled off lotsa feathers too." With that her eyes failed to focus and grew moist, while her dark cheeks seemed to pale.

I tried to swallow but managed only to cough. I had to look away before speaking, unable to calm the quaver in my voice.

"I'm so sorry. It must be hard, really hard for you."

"What? Well—I don't want—No." Sharon blinked a couple of times, and after she tightened her jaw, color surged back into her face, turning her lips to pink chocolate.

"I'll tell you one thing, he sure was one funky, fun-lovin' bird."

"Yeah, I'm sure he was, and there's no problem with getting another pet. After a little time passes, you could get a dog or, maybe, even an outside cat."

Sharon raised her head and favored me with a voluptuous smirk. "You doctors are so silly. You really think a dog is best for me?"

"I think a dog's a good idea, yeah."

At that her face broke into a supermodel's smile. "You doctors act like even a parakeet be a boogeyman bird, like he gonna give me the clap or Ebola or somethin' worse than what I already got."

"Well, with birds, there is a risk of psittacosis pneumonia, especially with AIDS patients."

"Yeah, that's it. I be so glad I didn't get the Sit-a-coast-most-us. I was worried to death 'bout that." Sharon was smiling but pressed her lips together, trying to suppress a laugh or cough or both. "I s'pose you doctors never take chances, never ever take off them latex gloves or break the cellophane around your T.V. dinners. You safe all the time, whether you be examinin' your patients or pettin' your dogs or gettin' freaky with your women."

Warmth pulsed through my face, and I shook my head, trying not to grin. "Well, don't throw me in with the doctors just yet. After all, I'm not wearing gloves, and I'm still a medical student." With that, I straightened my tie and stethoscope, lifted my chin.

"That's right, my bad. There be time for you, hope for you yet, 'cause you're young and dumb and tender, and — right now you only a —a —a wannabe." With the final word Sharon broke into bright, easy laughter that filled the room. I laughed so vigorously myself that I could scarcely breathe. I lost my balance, staggered, and almost dropped my stethoscope

A month later, I was on a different rotation and spending my time squinting at a computer screen or flipping through pages in *Harrison's Internal Medicine*. Only by chance did I hear of Sharon's catastrophic downturn and readmission to the hospital for what we called "comfort care." Was it only by accident that I wound up outside her room, staring at the door, and clutching my stethoscope like a life preserver?

As soon as I took a deep breath, it helped me relax, so I put on a smile before opening the door. I felt sure she would recognize me. She might strain to open her eyes, but I knew she'd smile big and bright and reach for my hand in a feeble attempt to thank me. Even now, even as sick as she was, I was positive her face would once again transfigure, making all thoughts sensual and all actions flirtatious.

She lay on her back with sheets up to her shoulders, her breath part light moan, part snore, part plaintive coo. The room smelled faintly of rubbing alcohol and urine. Seeing a bag for a urinary catheter hung on the bed frame, I asked myself whether this really was "comfort care." Comfort care, maybe, for the nurses who were exhausted and scared from changing an AIDS patient's bedding. Or comfort care for the family, to spare them the stench and knowledge that their loved one was dying between urine-soaked sheets.

I whispered "Sharon?" then immediately realized the sound of her breathing overwhelmed my voice. I smiled to myself, made a mental note to tease her about her snoring. I tried again with a much louder "Sharon?" and a gentle shake of her shoulder.

Suddenly, the room became still. Even the bustle in the hallway and clamor from the nurse's station fell away. The only sound was Sharon's faltering breaths, interspersed with a thumping that pounded louder and louder in my ears.

With my hand on her shoulder, I stood motionless and held my breath lest at any moment hers should stop. In the room's forbidding hush, my next attempt to awaken her was just as futile. Then I reached and tentatively touched Sharon's face, evoking no change, so I quickly withdrew my hand. When I spoke again, it was with a tight jaw and an angry tone.

"Sharon, you don't need a goddamn parrot. They probably did you a favor." Abruptly, I turned away and hurried out into the hall. There I rushed for the elevator, ignoring a passing nurse's smile. I walked stiffly, my jerky steps pounding a focus into my thoughts. Sharon is Black, I am White. She is fat, I am thin. She's 28, I'm 29. She is dying, I am not.

I groped for the elevator button without looking, and I don't remember stepping inside for the ride. I only remember how stifling the air was and how my finger wavered as I pressed my choice for a floor. The car moved, and I looked down to see my scarlet necktie seeming to spurt blood onto my white shirt. I felt I might suffocate, faint, or die if the elevator didn't stop soon. At last, the elevator flashed "1," the door opened, and I stepped into the hallway to exhale.

But people were approaching, and I needed to move. I tried to speed-walk but stumbled – a subtle but troublesome foot-drop that occurred in times of stress.

A colleague approached, far more peppy than needed at that late hour. "Hey, AIDS doc, why're you limping?"

I shrugged off the question with a nod, a wave, and roll of my eyes. I needed to rest, and a bathroom at the end of the hall offered sanctuary. Sharon's world revolved around some ominous letters: AIDS, HIV, PCP. My letters, MS, were something else, an annoying guest with too much to drink and too little savvy to leave the party, not violent but not really welcome either. Ignored, maybe nobody would notice.

And it was true that in the hospital's cool corridors, few noticed my intermittent limp or my avoidance of stairs. Nor could anybody see how heat affected me, how the midday sun stiffened my joints and hobbled my ability to move carefree along the beach. And there were other things that nobody noticed.

My pee tumbled into the bowl in uneven spurts, but my hand pressing below my bellybutton helped – no need for a catheter. Over the months, my bladder's mutiny had become worse, making restroom visits longer and more frequent. At times belly punches or silent curses epitomized my trips to the toilet, while at other times things worked and could be dismissed and forgotten like a bad dream.

With a smoother stride, I walked out of the restroom, down the corridor, and out of the hospital. The night air felt cool on my face, and I paused to close my eyes and inhale the scent of sea salt. I liked to sit by the ocean at night, listening, reveling in the stillness.

Suddenly, the coo of a mourning dove made me open my eyes and get back in motion. I couldn't remember whether the top deck of the hospital's parking garage overlooked the ocean, but hoping that it did, I climbed quickly and imagined myself racing to the summit of some majestic mountain.

Just above the fifth floor when I tried to run, my legs stiffened. I stopped to stretch and heard a dove's coo again. Out in the night, wind on the coastal hills made the eucalyptus trees undulate gently, dark specters of movement, quiet and haunting. And all of a sudden, there was Sharon in my mind's eye, alive – large brown breasts, dark eyes, that sleek smile.

"Sharon, you seem to be doing much better."

"Yeah, I ain't coughed my head off in at least five minutes." The smile flashed.

"Have you tried to walk?"

"Not yet. I been waitin' for someone to ask me before I walked down the aisle. Now if you be proposin' to me, I'll sure think 'bout it, but I can't promise nothin' 'cause I know you already married, and I ain't as wild as you medical people."

"Well, don't feel bad. Nobody's as wild as us medical people. Just try not to pine too much for me, while I'm away getting some help."

"I don't see why you be needin' help – a big strong man like yourself and a petite flower like me." She softened her tease with a giggle, and I left the room to find a nurse.

Minutes later, the nurse and I hoisted Sharon to her feet. Her legs shook from the strain, her breasts jiggled. Drops of sweat popped onto her forehead.

"Ooh, I be shaking it good now. Oh, shake it, baby." She collapsed back onto the bed, laughing.

"That's pretty good. Most dead people can't stand nearly that long or shake that well."

"Well, pretty soon, I'll be dancing down the hall, and Dr. Pearson—oh, sorry, I mean, Mr. Clint, the Medical Student, you'll have to dance with me."

"Okay, it's a date, Ms. Moore."

A couple days later, she not only danced down the hall, stopping briefly to sign forms, but continued out of the hospital into the southern California sunshine – gone, at least, for a month, and gone for the moment from my thoughts.

I began to climb the stairs again. Near the top deck of the garage, I rested, leaned on the railing, and whispered to myself. "Shake it, baby." I looked around the deserted deck to see that the only witness to my words had been a fleeting bird. There in the stillness, the night sounds played with my senses, growing louder in my head: the gentle rustle of trees, the dove's intermittent cooing, the rhythm of my own breath.

Above the rows of shadowy vehicles the night sky displayed its stars, inviting anyone to look up, to see the splendor, a sight far removed from doctors and hospitals and AIDS but, nonetheless, closer. I looked skyward, smiling, but could feel the tightness in my legs, and soon tears began rolling down my cheeks. I thought of Sharon, remembering her sass, her laugh, and the enticing flush of her lips, but, somehow, despite the night's mysteries, my tears were not hers, and the stars seemed to flicker with the sorrow of days yet to come.

Ursula

As a medical student, Clint often failed to distance himself emotionally from his patients. For example, when he began his clinical rotations, all his patients had AIDS, and he simply could not accept the fact that they were, for all intents and purposes, slated for death. Night after night, I heard stories of pneumonia not responding to antibiotics, cancer not responding to therapy, and a host of infections leading to paralysis, blindness, dementia, and death. It was not exactly pleasant dinner conversation.

The emotional strain on Clint was considerable, and time and again he attempted to make it through these tragedies either by denying their significance or by engaging in obsessive physical activity, such as the day he decided on the spur of the moment to ride his bicycle along the coast north of town.

At first I wasn't alarmed, for at the time Clint could manage a bicycle quite well. What I failed to consider was that his concept of "up the coast a ways" meant two hundred miles. So he rode for an entire day and night over rolling hills, through narrow streets and busy intersections. Around midnight some hooligans with paint guns drove by and shot him before speeding away. Clint managed to stay on his bicycle, but he came home with three hideous bruises on his back and a generous coating of bright yellow paint. And when I asked Clint why he did such things, his answer was, "For fun."

During those trying years, interspersed with Clint's "fun," I worked at a women's clothing store to do what I could to meet our financial obligations. Despite my salary and loans, grants, and scholarships, our credit card balance continued to grow. The cost of medical school and of life in Southern California was simply astonishing.

My hopes for a solution rested on Clint's future residency income, along with a lower cost of living in a smaller city. As usual, Clint left the money worries up to me. As a resident physician Clint would have enough worries, and so I tried not to add to his burden.

Clint

Bright and warm, the sunshine seemed to penetrate everything. I squinted in the light and smiled, a third-year student rotating through outpatient pediatrics. We medical students at my particular university rotated through various hospitals, research facilities, and community clinics, and today was my day at a military hospital's pediatric abuse clinic.

I studied my map and hoped I was heading right when my stride stiffened into a limp.

"Sir, are you okay?" It was a young naval ensign in a starchy, white uniform coming through the glass doors.

After I nodded, he went on his way at an impressive

clip.

When I restarted my stride improved and was almost normal by the time I reached my assigned clinic. There a nurse held the door for me, then a friendly woman with M.D. on her name tag came forward and stretched out a hand.

"You must be Clint. Welcome, I'm Susan Berkowitz. It's great to have you here." She smiled, and we shook hands. Her casual sweater, big sunglasses, and long curly hair, didn't look typical of a military physician.

"You're our first medical student in this clinic. As you might imagine, the issues can be pretty sensitive. There's not too much for you to do except watch, but I don't think you'll be bored. Our first patient should be here any minute."

"I'm sure I'll learn a lot." I exhaled and felt my shoulders relax. After long hours and intense rotations in medicine and surgery, I was tired of the strain. I was ready for a touchy-feely subject, even a little boredom.

"Where'd you go to undergrad?" The question took me by surprise, but I recovered quickly.

"Cal State Bakersfield, the paragon of prestige."

"Bakersfield? I didn't know they had a university."

"Yeah, it's small and pretty new."

"Did you find it hard to get into medical school, having gone to a small school?"

"I don't know. I mean, I got in and had several acceptances so I guess it worked out."

"That's good to hear. I thought medical schools, especially in the UC system, would discriminate against applicants from state colleges."

"Well, most of my classmates are from Berkeley or Stanford. Maybe somebody shuffled some papers the wrong way or got confused. Anyway, boom, here I am."

"I doubt it. Nobody gets in easy here. The ocean's here, and the weather's too good."

I didn't know how to respond, but then the receptionist entered. "First patient's here."

"Great. Send her back."

The door opened, and Dr. Berkowitz went to greet the

mother and child.

"Hi, my name's Susan Berkowitz."

"This is Clint, a medical student who's working with me. You must be the mother, Freda, and you must be Muriel. I'm so glad to meet you."

Dr. Berkowitz shook hands with both, but only Muriel smiled.

"I know this must be terribly difficult for you, but we'll make it as painless as possible. Let's go back here so we can talk."

At the end of the hallway, all three of them sat on a well-worn couch, while I found a chair and tried to blend into the wallpaper. When Muriel looked at me with dark, trusting eyes and smiled, I assessed her smiling. Cute kid. She seems to be doing well, probably here just because her mom is worried about some creep.

The mother, about thirty-five with puffy, pleading eyes, shifted, fidgeted, and bit her bottom lip. Her mouth opened but no words formed.

Dr. Berkowitz knew what to ask. "How old is Muriel?"

"She's nine now." The mother swallowed and tried to clear her throat.

Man, I was thinking, what is the matter with this mom, and will she be able to spit it out before time for dinner?

"How old was she when the abuse took place?"

"From age five until six months ago." At that the mother's breath quickened, and she clenched and unclenched her jaw several times before going on. "It was my fiancé. We broke up about six months ago so he wasn't around anymore. Then just last week Muriel told me what he did, what he had been doing to her." She looked up at the ceiling, then down before staring straight ahead and grinding her teeth. "I want to kill him." She shuddered and closed her eyes, squeezing out tears.

Dr. Berkowitz handed the mother a tissue as Muriel watched, visibly concerned.

What in the hell? Don't tell me some asshole molested this little girl. Man, I'm not ready to hear this.

"I know it's extremely hard, but it's not your fault. You're not the one who did this. He did it. He's to blame. Take a breath—relax—take another breath. Now, what did he do to her?"

"He had sex, intercourse, with my baby. How could he do that to a child, my child? I want to kill him. He's a monster, a monster." She trembled with fury, fighting to gain control until a cry burst from her throat and she dropped her tissue. She turned and took Muriel in her arms, and as they hugged, Muriel patted and stroked her mother's back.

For crying out loud, Pearson, stay cool. Hold it together. Be objective. The girl's safe now. She's okay.

"It's not your fault, Muriel. This guy was a bad guy. You did everything you could. You're very brave, very brave."

Muriel nodded but continued to rub her mother's back. Then she began to trace circles and other shapes, as if doodling in finger-paint.

Crap, this damn MS makes me emotional whenever I don't get enough sleep. I should have gone to bed sooner. Damn it, what was I thinking? Okay, a tear or two is no big deal. Just hold it together, Pearson, don't embarrass yourself.

"When the abuse started, did Muriel start acting strange or do anything different?"

The mother turned but continued to hold her daughter's hand. "She started wetting the bed. She had nightmares. She would wake up screaming. I didn't know what was wrong. I brought her here to see a psychiatrist, but he said everything was fine. I should have known. How could I not know? My baby was being hurt in my own home. How did I not know? How? HOW?"

She stared into space with glazed, dripping eyes. Her mouth was open, lips trembled, and tears began to stream down her face.

How come you didn't know? How come, damn it? Did he leave your bedroom and go to hers? It must have happened right under your goddamned nose. You should have known.

"He waited until I was gone to class. I was trying to get my AA degree, so I was taking evening classes. He would molest her after I left. He told her he'd kill her, and me, if she told. He told her it was her fault and that I'd be ashamed of her if I knew. Lies, lies! He's a monster! I let a monster hurt my baby. I'll kill him. I'll kill him!" Her hands tightened into fists, her fury into something worse.

"I should have known! Oh God, I should have known! It's all my fault, my fault. I should have known!" She gasped, twisted, and finally sank her face between her hands, sobbing.

I'm sorry. It's not you, not you, goddammit. It's not you. You were gone, you couldn't have known.

Dr. Berkowitz said the right things. "These guys are very good at hiding the truth. It's not your fault. There was no way for you to know. You didn't do anything wrong. Don't blame yourself. It is absolutely NOT YOUR FAULT. You didn't do this."

The mother kept her head down and began to rock back and forth in time with her tormented sobs. She seemed unable to hear and kept whispering, "No, no, no."

Muriel touched her head. "Mommy, Mommy, it's okay. I'm okay now."

The mother looked up, her eyes puffy, and just for a moment managed a smile, but within seconds that smile turned into a grimace, deep and tortured.

Okay, fuck it. Fuck the tears. I don't care about tears. Let's all cry real good, and then hunt this fucker down. I'd just love to introduce him to an Old Timer friend of mine.

I couldn't keep quiet any longer. "Where is this guy now? Is he in the Service?"

The mother turned slowly. "He's gone back to the Philippines, but he's not in the military."

Fuck . . . fuck.

Muriel tilted her head and looked at me.

Dr. Berkowitz came through again. "The most important thing is that you believe your daughter and help her through this, and I can already see that your daughter's going to do well. It's because you believe her and want to help. Everything will be all right, you'll see."

No. No. It can never be right. How can it be? Fuck.

Falling

Muriel and her mother embraced again, and for a minute or two, the only sounds were the mother's sobs and my own attempts to clear my throat. Eventually Muriel and her mother drew apart and Dr. Berkowitz handed the mother a new tissue.

"Mommy, it's okay now. I'm here and I don't have to pretend."

"What do you mean, pretend?"

"I used to pretend none of it was happening. I used to pretend I was in a castle far away."

Tears flooded the mother's face anew, but she wiped with the tissue and managed to speak. "You don't have to pretend anymore, sweetheart. You're safe, you'll always be safe."

Goddammit, make it true, make it true. It has to be true.

"What I need to do now is examine Muriel. Is that all right, Muriel, if your mom's there? I need to look you over in your private area, but it won't hurt. You'll need to take off your pants and panties and lie on this table, but it will be real quick, and I promise it won't hurt."

Muriel nodded, no apprehension on her face, and followed Dr. Berkowitz's instructions. She appeared comfortable lying on the table, holding her mother's hand.

Fuck. This is not something a nine-year-old should have to go through.

"This thing is a fancy light and microscope so I can see, and this metal thing also helps me see. If you are scared or uncomfortable at any time, all you have to do is let me know, and I'll stop immediately. Are you okay so far?"

"Yep."

"You're doing great. Only a little more and we'll be done. Are you having any pain?"

"No. I'm fine."

Muriel's mom squeezed her hand and whispered, "I love you."

"I love you too. It doesn't hurt. I'm fine."

"I'm sorry."

"Mommy, it's okay. I'm fine now."

The mother patted Muriel's hand and tried to smile, a forced, quivering grin.

"All done. You did great, Muriel. You can go ahead and get dressed. You are certainly very brave. We're all very proud of you."

In a few minutes everyone was back in place on the couch; I hadn't moved from my chair. The mother seemed calmer now, but she sat stiffly, waiting.

"From the exam, it's clear that this guy has had sex with Muriel, but you're okay, Muriel. You are still completely normal down there."

If I ever find this guy, he won't be normal down there ever again. Fuck . . . fuck.

The mother was crying again, quietly this time. Big tears rolled down her face and plopped onto her lap. She turned to Muriel. "I should have known. I won't ever let anyone hurt you again. Oh, ever, ever again, never. I promise. I love you so much."

Mother and daughter embraced but soon were able to let go, at least in part. They leaned their heads toward each other and held hands, slowly playing with each other's fingers.

Then it happened – a soft but distinct choking, throat-clearing sound. The mother looked up, nodded, and smiled. Muriel also looked at me and reached out toward me, her fingers waving slowly as if trying to stretch a little closer.

At least six feet away from the child, I closed my eyes but seemed to feel her smooth, light touch on my face, felt the tips of her moist fingers tracing down my cheeks, cooling, trying to soothe. Gentle as her touch might be, it only caressed the surface, could not burrow within, and could do nothing to dampen my rage.

CHAPTER EIGHT

Climbing through Residency

Clint

"Dr. Pearson, I'm scared. My mother's Deanna Rodriquez, and —" The young man turned away and shuddered, as if seeing something horrible. He looked to be about 17 or 18 years old, had on stylish clothes, and was so soft-spoken that the hallway conversations threatened to overwhelm his don't-tell-a-soul whisper.

"Carlos, it's all right. Your mom's one of my favorite patients. What's the matter?" I was cautious about revealing information about one of my AIDS patients. The community was conservative, and many still believed AIDS to be a disease of homosexuals. Here the diagnosis carried substantial stigma, and although I knew Deanna had told her family, I also knew the information was closely guarded, as closely guarded and shameful as "my brother molests little girls" or "my sister's hooked on heroin."

"My mom's all right now. I mean she's not sick or anything, but you're the one giving her medicine for AIDS, right?"

"Well, yeah, I'm treating her for AIDS, but fortunately we have good medicines that can extend her life. She just needs to be sure to take her medicines and keep seeing me regularly."

Carlos's shoulders relaxed. "That's what I want to talk about. Sometimes she has a stomachache and won't take her medicine, and sometimes she forgets. Can you be real strict with her and tell her she has to take her pills?" His eyes were moist, pleading.

"I've explained it to her a number of times, but I can certainly be more forceful. In fact, I'll read her the riot act." I smiled, hoping to ease his fears, but still he looked tense. Something else was there, some unspoken concern, and to reach it I'd have to coax it out. "Are you scared for your mom?"

"Yeah, of course. Also, she drinks a beer or two almost every day. You said she couldn't have any alcohol because of her medicines, but she doesn't listen." Carlos shifted in his seat and reached into his shirt pocket for a pack of menthol cigarettes.

"You can't smoke in here, and those things will kill you, anyway."

"Oh, I'm sorry, Dr. Pearson. I wasn't going to smoke." He dropped the pack in his lap as suddenly as if it were hot, then quickly slid it back into his pocket. "Dumb habit, sorry."

"Well, I'll definitely talk to your mom again about alcohol. She shouldn't drink at all. I don't want her pancreas to get irritated again." Uncertain of what more to say, I asked the next question slowly. "How's your relationship with your mom?"

"We get along good. She knows I love her, but you know, sometimes, well, sometimes, it's hard."

"What's hard? Do you two fight or argue a lot?"

"No, but sometimes— I mean, it's only natural. Sometimes I'm scared to hug her or drink after her or even talk to her about AIDS. I mean, you know, I don't want to get it."

"It's safe to hug your mom. There's absolutely no way you'll get HIV from that. As for drinking after her, you're probably not going to get HIV, but for sanitary reasons, it's not a good idea." I grinned. "As for talking, now, you'll definitely get AIDS from that."

Carlos's expression didn't change. "I don't really drink after her, and I do hug her a lot, but sometimes, you know, I'm still scared of getting HIV." He shrugged and shuddered again, reached toward his shirt pocket but stopped himself and twisted his hands aimlessly in his lap.

"We do get along good. She supports me. She really accepts me and my problems."

Falling

We were almost there, almost to the real issue.

"Look, Carlos, I'm not going to be judgmental. I don't care if you're gay or using drugs or both. I've got many gay patients and many drug-using patients. Sometimes I think you have to be one or the other or both to get into this clinic. It's okay. What are you doing that makes you so scared of getting HIV?"

After a poignant silence, Carlos raised his head. "I'm gay. It's so dumb. I can barely say it." He looked at me, then bit his lower lip. "I'm gay. But I've only had sex twice. I used condoms both times, but I'm still scared. I mean, so many gay guys are dying from AIDS, right? I've been tested three times, and I was negative each time, but I'm still worried about AIDS. It's crazy, but it's scary."

I nodded.

He attempted a feeble smile. "Can I still get it even if I used condoms? I mean the condoms never broke, but I don't know if the guys were positive or not. My dad says all fags will get AIDS. He hates me. We don't talk anymore. I'm scared. I've tried to stop having sex, but I can't do it. I don't know what to do."

A single tear rolled down Carlos's cheek before he broke down altogether, his body shaking, shedding many tears.

"Timeout – it's okay. Everything'll be all right." I handed Carlos a box of tissue and patted his arm.

The door was opening. "Dr. Pearson, I'm off. Sherri is your late nurse—oh, I'm sorry. I didn't mean to interrupt. Young man, are you okay?"

"Yeah, I'm okay, a little emotional." Carlos managed to smile and wiped away some tears.

"We always tell Dr. Pearson not to make his patients cry, but he never listens." She turned to me. "If you need a nurse, Sherri's still here."

"Karen, I don't think we'll need—" The door closed with a thud.

"I'm sorry, I didn't mean to freak out."

"It's okay. We have a lot to talk about, and, fortunately, you're the last patient so there's no rush. First, I don't care if you're gay. God made you gay, like he made me straight. Second, you do not have to get HIV just because you're gay, and finally, if you've been tested three times and you're negative, you're probably just that – negative. Now when were you last tested?"

"Three weeks ago."

"And when did you last have sex?"

"About, uh, seven months ago, I think. Yeah, seven months ago."

"Did you use a condom, and what kind of sex did you have?"

"Yes, we used condoms and only had oral sex."

"Did you perform oral sex on him, vice versa, or both?"

"Both, but I don't know if he was HIV positive or not."

"Condoms are extremely effective at preventing HIV, especially in oral sex, and in addition, you were negative six months later when you got tested. You just do not have HIV, Carlos, period."

His shoulders dropped, he smiled, and then he told me more. He stood in a no-man's land between disclosure and denial, the closet door half open, safe sadness within and dangerous freedom outside. He had stood there for years, not brave enough to defend who he was but not hypocritical enough to deny it. Most of his family covertly nudged or, sometimes, shoved him toward the closet, trying to hide his secret lest it reflect upon them and compel them to sit in the back pew at Our Lady of Mercy.

Only his mother, fighting an incurable disease, tried to coax him out. She spoke to him softly, as if he were an injured fox under her porch. Wild and beautiful and desperately needy, he cowered from the glare of disclosure yet longed for the joys of expressing most fully who he was. I knew it was only a matter of time. Someday soon his spirit would heal, nature would take its course, and the fox in Carlos would jump and play and forget to hide. I only hoped that when such a day came, despite shouts from beer-fueled cowboys, he'd turn, and in the brilliant light of midday not only stand his ground but learn to bite.

Falling

It was ten weeks before Carlos next visited the clinic, time for reflecting, accepting, ample time for change. On this visit Carlos was not the last patient, so a long encounter was neither possible nor needed.

"Hey, Carlos, how's it going?" I was enjoying the feel-good aftermath of delivering a healthy baby boy earlier that morning.

"Much better. I know you don't have a lot of time, but I want to let you know what's happening."

"I hope nothing's wrong."

"No. Everything's going good. My mom's healthy – knock on wood. I've got a new job, I'm getting my own place, and—" Carlos smiled. "I've met a guy. His name's Darren, and we're spending a lot of time together. He's HIV negative, but even so, we're having safe sex."

"That's great. That's fantastic. I was afraid you'd say you had started drinking heavily, picking fights, and torturing small animals in an attempt to become straight."

"Nope, no such luck. I'm a recovering heterosexual, not practicing."

We both laughed, but Carlos was eager to tell me more. "I met Darren right here in town. He was so cute I couldn't stand it. He was already out, otherwise, I'd never have had the guts to ask him on a date. After that, everything sort of fell into place. Now I've introduced Darren to my family. Mom likes him. The others aren't sure, but I like him, and that's all that matters."

"You're right. Does this mean you're out of the closet?"

"Definitely. So far, the only one who's been an asshole is my dad, but even he hasn't been all that bad. I guess I'm a big disappointment to him." He frowned, then shrugged. "A couple of friends have stopped coming around, but I figure that's their problem."

"A lot more family members and friends may come around if you give them time, but on the other hand, I wouldn't let anyone be mean to you."

"I won't. If they don't like that I'm gay, too bad."

"I can't believe how much you've changed. You look so much more confident and happy."

"I feel good." Carlos laughed, scratching the back of his head. "Darren's helped me a lot."

"I can see he's had a wonderful effect on you, but I'm sure you've done a lot of it on your own. Be sure you give yourself credit."

"It was all a matter of timing. Darren came along when I was sick of hating myself."

"Sometime you'll have to introduce me to Darren."

"Would you really like to meet him?"

"Of course."

"Then I'll bring him by."

I remembered one more thing I wanted to say. "Carlos, by all means keep practicing safe sex. Now that you're happier and out, you may have a tendency to throw caution to the wind, and whether you're straight or gay, it's important to protect yourself."

"Don't worry. No glove, no love." He grinned. "Darren and I agree on that." Then his demeanor became serious. "I want to say thanks, Dr. Pearson, for listening to me and helping me. Also, before I go would it be all right, if — "

"If what?"

"This is going to sound dumb, but would you mind if I gave you a hug?"

I grinned right back at him. "Well, I heard one time that all gays have AIDS, but I suppose one hug won't hurt."

One hug it was, brief but sufficient to bridge, if only for a moment, the gulf between human worlds.

As he got up to leave, I pointed toward the pack of cigarettes peeking from his shirt pocket. "At the next visit we need to get you off those things."

"Hey, that's what Darren says. Anyway, I'll probably see you again in a couple weeks when my mom comes in. I figure somebody has to keep her in line."

With that, Carlos waved goodbye to walk out with a new lightness in his step.

Now at the stage of my work that required a descriptive code on the billing sheet, I found this one a poser. While I knew I'd done something important, something as great as delivering a baby or making a tough diagnosis, I didn't know how to code this particular something. So after several half-hearted attempts I crumpled the paper and tossed it in the trash, unaware that the work was just beginning.

"I broke out in hives, Dr. Pearson." Deanna's lips trembled.

"When did this happen?"

"Yesterday." Carlos answered for her.

Red skin and blisters covered Deanna's face and arms, and although her lips were only a little swollen, her peeling, wet-crusted nostrils flared below her bloodshot eyes.

"Where else do you have the rash?"

She shook her head. "Everywhere, everywhere." She pulled back clothes to reveal more angry skin.

"Did you take any new medicines, change soap, eat something new, get into any poison oak?"

"No, nothing new."

"Is it itchy?"

"Yes, but not as bad as poison oak."

"Are you short of breath?"

"A little, and my mouth and tongue feel swollen."

"When did you last take your Bactrim?"

"This morning. I've been good at taking it."

I shook my head. "This is probably from the Bactrim. As you know, you need to take the Bactrim to prevent PCP, *Pneumocystis* pneumonia, but now you won't be able to take it for a while. We may be able to desensitize you to Bactrim or give you something else to prevent PCP, but either way you need to come in the hospital."

"How dangerous is this?" Carlos was holding his mother's hand.

"The rash will go away in time, and the chances of her getting PCP before we get her on something else should be small. However, if things get worse and a large amount of skin starts peeling, it can get complicated, sort of like a bad burn. I also want to get her in and out of the hospital quickly so she doesn't catch some bad hospital bug."

I turned from Carlos to Deanna. "I'm sorry, I know you're miserable."

"I can't sleep. I toss and turn, and I'm weak."

"I'll get you some medicine to make you feel better. Also, this may have been caused by one of your other medicines, not the Bactrim, so we'll need to stop all of them."

"Won't the AIDS get worse?"

"We hope not, if we don't keep you off the medicines too long, but I won't lie to you, it makes me nervous. On the medicines your T-cell count has gone from eleven to almost a hundred, and I'd hate for us to lose ground."

"I know you're my doctor, and I trust you, but is this something you deal with?"

"I've dealt with this before, and I've dealt with it in AIDS patients. You have an allergic reaction, possibly a problem called Steven-Johnson syndrome, but I'll be talking with AIDS experts and dermatologists, people smarter than me. Also, you'll have a whole team of doctors — an intern, an attending physician, and me."

"Did your other AIDS patients with this problem do — do okay?" Deanna's voice broke on the last word.

"They all lived. You're going to do fine, but your smooth complexion and modeling career may be messed up for a while."

"Not my modeling career, I just lost two pounds." Deanna rubbed her wide hips and started to laugh, at first a giggle, then morphing into loud, sleep-deprived sobs, the kind that bring substantial relief but can also make it hard to breathe.

The next day I found Deanna in the hospital.

"Is the medicine helping your itching?" I winced, remembering when I myself had a severe case of poison oak.

"A little. I was able to sleep a few hours, but the rash is still bad. See?" Deanna removed clothing to reveal blisters and a rash that had changed little.

"How about your mouth?"

"Not too bad." She opened her mouth and stuck out her tongue playfully.

"How about your vaginal area?"

"It's okay, not any worse, only the usual gonorrhea, herpes, and syphilis."

I smiled but became serious. "I talked to two different dermatologists. One said we should definitely give you prednisone, and the other said we should definitely not give you prednisone. Needless to say, it's an area of some controversy."

"What do you think?"

Suddenly, I remembered that I myself was taking prednisone, and doing so in secret, compliments of a Tijuana pharmacy. It had started innocently enough. While in medical school, I had "prescribed" myself a ten-day course of prednisone to treat my worsening stiffness, but as I tapered off the dosage my symptoms had come back, and I prescribed myself another round of pills. The prednisone energized me and helped me to walk without too much of a limp. I needed it, I told myself, to treat my MS, and although I always meant to get off the medicine for good, the time was never quite right. I was always on a tough rotation, or facing exams, or just having some fresh trouble with walking or standing or peeing. I already knew, of course, the long-term effects of prednisone – osteoporosis, poor healing, diabetes, infections, broken bones – but no time seemed right to give it all up and—

"Dr. Pearson?"

"Deanna, yeah, sorry, I think we should wait and only give you prednisone if it gets worse."

"Okay. It's not getting worse so far. Knock on wood."

"I also spoke with a couple of AIDS experts. They agreed that the Bactrim was probably the culprit and recommended that we undertake desensitization in a few weeks or so. That's where we give you a small dose of Bactrim and gradually increase the dose to get your body used to it. However, they warned that this could happen again, even after you're desensitized."

"Isn't there another medicine you can give me, instead of Bactrim?"

"There are other meds, but they don't work as well. The experts thought it best to avoid any new medicines right now with you. They felt the risk of PCP was small as long as we get you back on Bactrim in the near future."

"What about my AIDS medicines?"

"Everyone I spoke to agreed that you should be all right without them for a while. Some of those medicines can cause this problem, and we need to wait before we reintroduce them."

"How much longer will I be here? The food's terrible."

"Probably a day or two more. Have Carlos or Darren bring you some home-cooked food. Speaking of the dynamic duo, have they been around?"

"Yeah, you just missed them. I'm worried about Carlos, though. He was doing so much better, but now this seems to have thrown him for a loop. He's smoking more. If I die, I don't know how he'll take it."

"I'll talk with him, but, more importantly, I better not let you die." I smiled, as if I really had such power.

Sometimes a lifetime of study leaves one incomplete, unsure, even ignorant as to the best course of action. Sometimes the experts are wrong, even when they recommend a treatment with confident pride. Always the unpredictable can occur, and, yes, sometimes a faint, unsettling feeling arises, an invisible tug of the sleeve that says, "Ignore the standards, the studies, and the specialists. Listen to your intuition."

Fifteen days after discharge from the hospital Deanna was back. Her sweat-streaked face told the story of fever, cough, and a progressive battle to breathe. Her symptoms had started innocently enough: a dry throat (too much yelling at the baseball game), some gasping during exercise (just out of shape), and feeling warm (thermostat's up too high). But by the time she came to the clinic her chest was heaving, her mouth open, and despite her resolve to appear strong before Carlos, fear shimmered in her eyes. It was an easy call.

"Get a wheelchair and let's get her to the E.R. NOW."

"Why do I (gasp) have to go to (gasp) the E.R.?"

"Deanna, we'll be able to treat you better over there. You may have to be intubated."

"What's —"

"That's where we put a tube in your mouth and down your windpipe so you can breathe better. GET A

WHEELCHAIR!"

"Does it—does it hurt?"

"It's uncomfortable, but if we do that, we'll give you medicine so you'll be asleep or very groggy."

"Do what" (gasp) "you have to."

"Try not to talk. Save your energy. GET A WHEELCHAIR!"

Carlos took the opportunity to speak. "It'll be fine, Mom. Try to relax."

A nurse arrived with a wheelchair, looking more terrified than Deanna or Carlos, and I rolled Deanna to the E.R. as fast as my stiff legs would go. The E.R. clerk saw us coming and opened the door, motioning to Carlos to stay behind.

In seconds the E.R. nurses had an oxygen mask on Deanna's face and a pulse oximeter on her finger. The oxygen sensor flashed 81%, beeped in alarm, and two E.R. doctors hustled into the room to listen.

I offered a quick summary. "This is Deanna Rodriquez. She has AIDS, and her Bactrim was discontinued about three weeks ago secondary to Steven-Johnson syndrome. The plan was to desensitize her to Bactrim, but she's obviously in respiratory distress now. Deanna, how long have you been short of breath and running fevers?"

"A week" (gasp) "or so."

I listened to Deanna's lungs while the nurses started an I.V and the senior E.R. physician, Dr. Nelson, gave some orders. "We need a STAT chest x-ray, ABG, and let's get set up to intubate. How's she sound, Dr. Pearson?"

"She's got crackles."

"Have you talked to her about intubation?"

"Yes, she's okay with it."

Dr. Nelson listened to Deanna's lungs and was joined by a grass-green intern named Francine Betters. A brand-new physician, she looked apprehensive, while Dr. Nelson seemed to welcome this break in routine – some real E.R. work in between sore throats, running noses, and Oxycontin-seeking patients.

"Dr. Betters, I'd like you to get ready to intubate this patient."

"Okay." She blinked several times before reaching for the laryngoscope and endotracheal tube.

After orders were given for sedation, everything appeared ready.

I laid a hand on Deanna's shoulder. "It's okay, Deanna. We're going to give you medicine to make you go to sleep and then we'll put the tube down your throat. It'll be okay."

Deanna nodded, and her body seemed to melt into the gurney as the nurse delivered the drugs. A respiratory therapist (RT) held an Ambu bag over Deanna's mouth and nose and squeezed, forcing oxygen into her lungs. The oxygen sensor flashed 88%.

Francine placed the laryngoscope in Deanna's mouth, sweeping the tongue out of the way, and pulled the scope up and forward. Her technique appeared perfect, but she shook her head.

"86% . . . 83% . . .79%." The RT announced the oxygen readings.

Francine withdrew the laryngoscope, and the RT got busy with the bag. The oxygen sensor flashed 81%, 83%, then 85%, but that was as far up as it would go. Francine tried again with the same result, except this time the oxygen level stuck at 83%.

Dr. Nelson said, "Let Clint get in there. You'll get the next one."

The RT reported, "83% sat."

I replaced the laryngoscope in Deanna's mouth and lifted up and forward. The vocal cords were so obvious that I wanted to take the endotracheal tube straight in, but a nurse placed it in my right hand backward. For most physicians this would have been inconsequential, not so for me. With the laryngoscope in my left hand, I kept the cords in view and clumsily attempted to reposition the endotracheal tube with my right.

"81%."

I got the tube turned, pushed it toward the cords.

"79%."

The tube was in, the bag attached.

Falling

"83% . . . 86% . . . 89% . . . 92%."

I gave a resounding "Yes" and exhaled.

"Nurse, please give Dr. Pearson five milligrams of Valium." Dr. Nelson was only teasing, but it sounded like a great idea.

Deanna's chest was x-rayed and blood drawn as the RT, now looking bored, squeezed the bag regularly to force oxygen into her lungs.

"So, Dr. Betters, what's your diagnosis?" Dr. Nelson was the one asking.

"Pneumonia, probably a typical bug. I'd think PCP would be unlikely since she's only been off Bactrim for a short time."

"Dr. Pearson?"

"I'd agree, but I'm still worried about PCP."

After we worked out a treatment plan, Dr. Nelson said, "Okay, then. Dr. Pearson, if you'll check the chest x-ray, Dr. Betters and I will write some orders and work on getting your patient upstairs."

"No problem."

When I began walking, Dr. Nelson noticed my stiff gait. "What's the matter?"

"Oh, I've got MS, and my legs sometimes take a while to relax."

"I didn't know that." Concern showed on his face.

"Yeah, I've told several people, but, I guess, they need to gossip more." I restarted, my stride now a little better.

Just outside the E.R., however, I stopped to stretch. I needed a break and thought about a mountain climb that I had scheduled in three months time. I stroked my thighs, imagining. It'll be great as long as my legs hold up.

In the radiology department with Deanna's film up on the lighted panel, I saw that the endotracheal tube was in the correct place, but I didn't like the web of whitish markings I saw—as if a child had taken white paint to draw an intricate pattern of reticulations and half-letters. The disease was so extensive that only the area above the diaphragm remained dark.

"Oh, shit."

* * *

"Here's what I'm going to do. I'll shimmy up the crack in this rock. You need to find the footholds. They're good footholds, so if your feet are slipping, they're in the wrong spots." My nephew David listened impassively. "Then I'm going to the left, over to the crack across the rock. See it? I'll put my feet in it and follow it around to the right." I nodded, approving my own plan. Rocks helped my MS, allowed my arms to work, taking the pressure off my shaky legs.

David looked unsure. "Should we get or do we need, you know—the rope?""Not unless we make a mistake. Now after the crack, I'll be in that upside-down vee area, and I'll walk up it with my feet in the bottom and my hands on either side. At the top, I'll reach for that ledge, it's a good handhold. Then I'll hand-over-hand it to the right and squeeze between that overhang and the rock floor. Got it, David?"

"Yeah, yeah, I'll watch you." David was squinting in the late-afternoon sun.

"Okay, then. Here goes." I did nearly all of what I'd described, then motioned to David to start.

He struggled with the first part until he planted his feet in the right spots. Then after climbing up the left side of the rock, he had difficulty following the crack to his right. "Damn, how'd you get your feet in here?"

"Just try to get the tips of your boots in, not the whole foot, and the crack gets wider as you go. Take your time. Be sure of every move." I forced myself to keep my voice slow and calm.

David negotiated the crack and soon stood between two rocks that angled together in the shape of an upside-down V. With his boots wedged in the center and his hands touching the granite sides for balance, he climbed up until he faced a smooth wall of stone. Then he looked upward, tottered, and had to duck his head to regain stability.

"Whoa, I gotta be careful."

"Take your time. You can do it."

He stretched his body flat against the rock face, reaching overhead for a handhold, but he hesitated, frowning at the smooth wall to his right. "Now what?"

"Concentrate on the handhold. The wall's too slick for your feet, but the handhold's good. Just work your way to the right and go under this overhang on your belly."

Apprehensive, I watched him with little more to offer than advice.

David moved right, hoisted himself onto a limestone ledge, and crawled under the overhang. Inch by inch, his chest pushed forward and upward, brushing against flaky granite, pebbles, and dust.

He lifted his head, trying to see, and hit it on the rock. "Damn, not enough headroom." Before he could say more, he was in the clear, standing and brushing dust from his clothes. "Where to now?"

"Right up there." I indicated the direction with my head. "We're almost done, but rest. The next part is vertical. Don't be in a hurry to die."

Still standing, he looked at the rock, then back at me, took a deep breath, and realigned his body as a sign he was ready to try. I had to smile. "Okay, this next part is straight up, but there's a perfect handhold. It's just a matter of doing a pull-up."

I stepped forward, grabbed a wide overhead ledge, and pulled myself to the top. David's short stature made the move more difficult for him, and even after finding the handhold and pulling partway up he dangled, gritting his teeth.

"There's a foothold on your right."

"Shit, where the hell you — oh, I got it." With that he made it to the top where a collection of loose boulders baked in the sun. "Yeaaaaah, man! Wooooo!" His yell echoed off the cliffs as he grabbed a fist-sized rock and flung it. Several seconds later, a faint cracking sound broke the silence. David grinned, threw another, then another, and watched each rock fly through the air before disappearing with a crack or a thud.

As for me, I stood alongside him squinting in the sunshine and surveyed the scene. Near the top of the mountain, lofty pines and cliffs captured the afternoon sun, dwarfing the boulders, slides, and deadfalls. Further down, black-oak thickets on the foothills and upper valleys stayed clear of the smoggy haze in the grasslands of the valley floor.

I had to caution David, who was still throwing rocks.

"Be careful not to throw yourself off. I'd have a hard time explaining it to your mom. Think you can see Durban from up here?"

He nodded and sat down. "Almost."

I wanted to keep the conversation going. "So, how were the schools in South Africa?" At that, David's dark face tightened.

"Not too bad if you liked being caned." He rubbed his neck, grimaced, and reached for another rock.

"Why'd they cane you?" I couldn't imagine David as unruly, even if it was years ago.

"I don't know – a lot of things, anything. Nothing." He stood and went back to his rock-hurling.

"I hear you have a new girlfriend."

"Yeah, Yvonne, she's great." He grinned. "I wish I could get her up here." He looked toward the horizon and the lowering sun, and as we both stood quiet, the only sound was of the wind whistling against the rocks and through the gaps

"We better get out of here before the sun sets. We don't want to be still climbing in the dark. We'll spend the night on the ridge, then take on Dennison Mountain tomorrow."

"You mean this isn't Dennison?"

"This is Dennison Peak." I pointed to the east, a larger peak. "That's Dennison Mountain. Now, David, getting down is harder than getting up. Take your time and be sure of every move.

David did and an hour later we reached our previous campsite.

"Hey, David, your pack's waiting for you, and it looks like the bears didn't even eat your food, although they might have pissed on your sleeping bag."

David lifted the pack but didn't hoist it over his shoulders. "How much farther?" He sounded like he was running out of steam.

"Better put it on. I figure we'll go a bit before we call

it quits. Anything we do now, we don't have to do in the morning." I tried to sound fresh, but I was limping and my gait was stiff.

The air was cooling, the light fading, and we soon came to a relatively level saddle with lush grass and ferns. Beyond it towered Dennison Mountain, its rock slides, timber, and wind-twisted bushes barely visible in the dying light.

"Here's where we'll camp." I dropped my pack.

"Good. I think I got blisters."

We opened our packs and strewed their contents onto the ground, but as night came on, so did unwelcome guests.

David slapped his arm, then his forehead. "Damn, these mosquitoes are bad."

"No kidding." I hunkered down, trying to cover my head. "Grab a bite to eat, then we'll take cover in our bags."

We soon found we'd chosen our campsite poorly, proof that experienced mountaineers can make novice mistakes. The damp surroundings generated swarms of mosquitoes, and on a warm summer night huddling in a down sleeping bag would soon become a sweaty, suffocating business. We needed at least a tiny gap to breathe, but the determined bloodsuckers found every opening.

At first the sleeping bag seemed inviting, but I was at the very edge of sleep when an extra bead of sweat rolled down my cheek and my own hot breath rolled back into my face. Feeling ready to smother, I couldn't stand it and hastily emerged from the bag.

For a little while, the cool air felt refreshing and the buzzing seemed inconsequential, but then the demons began to bite and I began to slap and itch. When I'd had enough, it was back into the bag, shortly afterward I came out again, and the cycle continued deep into the night.

"Man, Clint, these damn mosquitoes are killing me."

"I'm not doing any better. Hang in there. Eventually it'll get cool enough to stay in our bags."

By the time it got cool enough the mosquitoes had vanished, yet we both wound up scratching until dawn. At sunrise, mosquitoes still at bay, David and I ate in silence except for my occasional cusswords aimed at nothing in particular.

After we'd loaded our packs, we both came to life again, though our dispositions improved little.

I hoisted my pack to my shoulders, while glaring at Dennison. My MS was always much less of a problem in the morning. "Hey, David, you ready to kick this big fucker in the ass?"

"Yeah. I'm ready."

Within minutes we'd come to a precipitous grade where the work was exhausting, and one misstep promised a long, rapid fall. After an hour, we stopped to rest, heads down, sucking in the cool, thin air.

"Man." David panted and looked up the ridge, almost stumbling backward as he did so. "Do we have to do this?"

I shrugged, trying to smile in between breaths. "Yeah."

The next hour was like the first until we encountered bushes that crippled our already slow pace. Flat rocks near the top let us move at a better pace, and from that vantage point, Dennison Peak behind and below us looked like a trivial collection of ridge rocks, hardly worth climbing.

At the top we rested, scanning the mountainside. Before us, the canyon dropped sharply into a rugged mass of logs, loose boulders, and bushes, and farther below a stand of cedar swayed in the wind.

I hollered in triumph down the canyon. "WOOOO! Get out of our way, bears! We're coming through."

David couldn't match my volume, although he managed a breathy "Woooo, bears."

Our descent was rapid and uneventful until the trees gave out and a sixty-foot slide of near-vertical rock tumbled into the gorge.

I moved to my right, climbing down the rocks cautiously and issuing periodic
warnings to David. After thirty minutes of wary descent, thirty minutes of balancing and
triple testing handholds, we stopped. The gorge plummeted before us – a narrow crack
twisting downward into the chasm. We could see no

other routes, and retreat, always a theoretical consideration, ranked on my personal scale somewhere between unnecessary caution and head-bowed cowardice.

"Okay, let me go first. If I fall and die, you should probably try another route."

"Are you sure?"

"No, on second thought, you might want to try the same course even if I fall and die." I set my jaw, forced my hands into a crack, and swung my feet off the side. To my relief, my feet found a niche, and I began a methodical descent. Although I could only feel the footholds, I could see exactly where to wedge my hands, and twenty feet further, the rock flattened enough that I could see the footholds too, but not for long. Ten feet lower, the rock slanted more steeply and once more hid the footholds from my sight.

I did my best to keep cool, aware of David watching from above. "No problem." I dislodged my left hand to take a lower grip, but just then my feet slipped. I grappled for a hold but could only claw uselessly at the granite. I was falling, twisting, dangling only by my right hand or, more accurately, my right ring finger, which was buried in a crack. I howled in pain and fought for footing.

Twice I seemed to have a foothold, only to slide again and swing from my right hand. Choked with panic, I found new strength and managed to lift my body and kick. As my right boot stuck in a crack, I wriggled my left hand into a fissure, then with my body shaking, closed my eyes and pressed my forehead against the rock.

"Hey, are you okay down there?" David's voice sounded a long way off.

I cursed under my breath, then hollered up, "Yeah, I'm okay now. I almost fell off this fucking rock. Stay where you are. Do not try to climb down this way. I REPEAT. DO NOT CLIMB DOWN THIS WAY."

After pulling my right hand from its crack, I found my ring finger swollen, bleeding, and bent outward at the first joint. Blessedly, it still would function, and I shook it before reaching for a new grip.

Fifteen minutes later after a tedious, talk-out-each-move descent, I was at the foot of the cliff, straining to see David who now seemed ridiculously far away.

"David, work your way over to your right, to that tree. You can tie the rope to that tree and get part way down using the rope."

"What tree? I don't see a tree."

"It's over to your right. Just work your way over there. Be very careful." Oh God, please don't let him fall. Do not let him fall.

"I see the tree. I think I can get there."

"Be careful. Take your time."

Then David was beside the tree, pulling out the rope. "How strong is this rope?"

"Strong enough." I hope. "Just tie it tight, lots of knots."

"How long is it?"

"Thirty feet. It'll get you halfway." Well, a good third, anyway. "It gets less steep after that."

David tied knot after knot.

"That's good. Now use the rope to carefully climb down."

"Just a few more knots."

God, please, don't let him fall. Please, don't let him fall.

David started down, tentatively at first, then seemed to gain confidence. He had a minor slip but steadied himself with the rope. Lower, slowly lower, he moved.

Grotesque and dark, the possibilities were like childhood's nighttime monsters. Grown up, I could only face them with the help of humor. I swallowed, imagining the conversation with David's mother. Sorry, Charm, David fell off a cliff and died. I had no choice but to leave his mangled body on a rock in some godforsaken canyon. Don't worry, though, I managed to say a few words for him, and he didn't die in vain, because he'd already reached the summit of Dennison Peak. Furthermore, his chocolate-covered granola bars helped me make it home. I thought about him every time I took a bite.

David slipped again, regained his footing.

"Take your time. Be sure of every move." Please, God,

Falling

don't let him fall. Oh, don't let him fall.
David reached the end of the rope – my stomach knotted. He continued to work his way downward, moving slowly. At a difficult spot he sat down and kept coming on his bottom.
"Hold it, David! You need to turn toward the mountain. If you start sliding on your butt, you'll never stop."
"Okay, okay. Don't worry. I'll make it."
And he did. In a few moments, he was down, sitting on a log and shaking his head. While he looked exhausted and said no more, I felt exuberant and offered him every candy, cookie, and granola bar in my pack.

"It looks pretty good from here, at least, for a while. You might survive this trip after all, David." A small stream twisted down the gorge, and the walking looked relatively easy. "Just don't step on a rattler, and GET OUT OF OUR WAY, BEARS." My shout echoed off the canyon walls. "I'VE GOT A .44 MAGNUM, AND I'LL SHOOT YOUR DICK OFF."
When we came to a familiar pool of clear, cold water we rested, drinking our fill and eating granola bars when suddenly David's face changed.
"Shouldn't we be treating this water or something? Can't we get *Giardia*?"
"It depends. Who carries most of the *Giardia*?"
"I don't know."
"People and cows, beavers and otters. Do you see any trails, roads, people, campers, cows, otters, or beavers around here?"
"No."
"Well, it's actually not quite that simple. Deer and bear and other animals can carry *Giardia,* but in a place like this where there's nothing above us screwing up our water, our chances of getting *Giardia* aren't that great. Besides, I've drunk this water dozens of times, and I've never had a problem."
"Okay, then." David threw a stick toward the stream.
"Then again, not everyone who carries *Giardia* is symptomatic. It could be that I'm one of the lucky few who

doesn't have a problem with it, and it could be that at any moment, you'll develop severe abdominal cramps, horrendous, smelly diarrhea, and will probably die. The only good news is that you'll probably be too stinky for the bears to eat."

"Ha, ha." David rolled his eyes and put on a fake grimace before his next swig of water. "Best bear poop and *Giardia* I've ever had."

I chuckled and closed my eyes, appreciating the sound of the water and the whisper of wind in the pines.

Soon we were moving again, easily, lazily – a daydreamy descent through short ferns and tall pines. Thoughts of home crept into my mind: Pepsi at the poolside, the pop of the can and the bubbling fizz as it splashed over ice, barbecued steak sizzling and splattering, a hot fluffy French roll, corn on the cob dripping with golden butter. All the while, brown-skinned figures flitted and flirted around me, plying me with more and more food, smiling, seemingly unmindful of their bouncing breasts and seductive hips, at least, until we were alone, undressed, and the brown eyes invited me to—

A deep grunting growl broke my daydream, and I saw a pair of eyes, frozen intensity beneath a fury, furrowed brow.

"Oh, shit, there he is, David."

I slowly removed my pack, opened the flap, and started to reach for my .44 Magnum, but before I could grab the pistol, the bear turned and ambled away. With a big "Whew!" I stopped rummaging and decided to hurry the bear along. "Get on out of here, bear!" I yelled. The effect was immediate but not what I wanted.

About thirty yard away by then, the bear turned back, jumped over a three-foot-tall manzanita bush, and charged. Now I had no choice. Grabbing the pistol was urgent. Next time, stupid, get the gun in your hand, *then* yell at the bear.

The bear was closing the distance—thirty yards, twenty, ten, then five by the time I had the gun in my hand and cocked. As the bear stopped short, the gun blasted and the bear lurched forward, crumpling to the ground dead.

A lucky shot had pierced the bear's heart, but then I saw something worse. Two cubs suddenly raced toward their dead mother, wailing as if shot themselves. Before reaching her body, they stopped, retreated, and scampered up a tall pine. Higher and higher, they spiraled around the tree, continuing to growl and cry.

"Damn." David looked stunned.

I was too. "Oh, God, that's why the bear charged. She had cubs. Fuck. I just couldn't put on the brakes. Damn it. I doubt they'll survive without their mother"

Already they were so high in the tree that they were difficult to see among the limbs, but we could still hear their growls.

I sighed. Maybe they were big enough to scrounge berries and ants, catch snakes, stumble across a dead, maggoty squirrel. Maybe they could find enough berries to keep moving, enough bugs and worms, enough protein and fat to live and grow and learn.

David was smiling, shaking his head. "I can't believe we killed a bear. Man, that bear moved fast. I can't believe it."

In the quiet that followed, time seemed to distort, twist in the tangled pain of my memories. I walked over to the dead body, then stood looking down at it before closing my eyes.

Her brown eyes stared upward, unblinking, frozen like those of a department-store mannequin. Her dirty-blonde hair hung matted about her shoulders. Her mouth was still open, her lips a grotesque grin around the endotracheal tube. The I.V. in her left hand had slipped from its vein, and her hand was slowly swelling like a fighter's after a misplaced hook, only now the fight was over.

Just moments before, the urgent activity, the chest pounding had ceased, and in the silence that followed, doctors and nurses and note-takers shuffled out of the room. Before she hurried out, one nurse remembered to cover Deanna's bare chest, leaving me to stare at a silent monitor.

After some time I looked down and stroked Deanna's stringy hair. Still on automatic-doctor, I listened to her chest, shone a light in her eyes, closed them, and slowly walked out to the visitor's lounge where Carlos sat alone, elbows on knees, staring at his shoes.

Another hand on another shoulder. "I'm so sorry, Carlos. She's gone. We did all we could, but it was no use."

"I know. You did what you could." He still didn't look up. A couple of tears fell onto the floor next to his shoes. I sat down and put my arm around him, but he didn't break down, didn't collapse into hysterical sobs. Instead, he turned and looked at me, wiping his eyes. "Can I see her?"

Once in the room, Carlos sat on the bed next to his mother, holding her hand and talking to her. "Mom, you're the best. I love you, but it's okay. I'm going to miss you, but you stayed as long as you could. All of us will be all right and . . ."

I slipped out of the room and found Deanna's chart, Carlos's eulogy still faintly audible from the ICU. "Shit, shit, shit," I said, for no one's benefit but my own, then settled down to write a businesslike summary for the chart.

Pt with AIDS/PCP, on vent x 1wk with slow deterioration, had
sudden code into asystole. Atropine and epinephrine given along
with CPR but no response. Code called. No heartbeat, no respiration, eyes fixed and dilated. No oculocephalic
reflex.

Soon Darren arrived, quietly entered the room, and sat down next to Carlos, who. paused long enough to extend his free hand – a warm touch to make up for the cooling one? In a perfect world, the two lovers would have spent those solemn moments crying together, talking, hugging, even coaxing a smile from each other, but all too often life requires immediate action, even a ferocious and untimely defense.

Another young man in khakis and white T-shirt entered the room. He had short, crew-cut hair, scowling lips, a muscular build. Despite his rugged looks, he was shorter and smaller than Carlos and took great pains to avoid looking at Deanna. He was Carlos's cousin, a distant cousin in more ways than one.

"Carlos, don't you think it would be better to have

only family here? A whole bunch of people are coming, and I don't think they'll be too thrilled with your boyfriend." He emphasized the word "boyfriend" and rolled his eyes.

Darren moved to stand up. "That's fine. I'll step out."

"No, Darren, you're not going anywhere. Larry, this is my partner, Darren. He's a part of the family and has every right to be here. Besides, I need him here."

"I'm trying to think about how it will look. Don't you have any shame? Do you really want to parade your fag boyfriend before the family at a time like this?"

"You don't seem to have a problem parading your slutty girlfriend before the family."

"Why would I? She's normal, and who you calling slutty?"

Carlos's jaw and hands clenched as he stood up. "My mom never liked you. She thought you were an asshole. You know what? You are an asshole. You have no right being here. Get out. Get out of this room right now."

Carlos's eyes were red, tear-filled. He lunged, swinging wildly at Larry, but Larry dodged, backed out of the room, and disappeared down the hallway, yelling. "You're crazy, you and your fag boyfriend." He was down the hall before Carlos could pursue.

"Fuck you, asshole!" Carlos's chest was heaving, but he clearly wasn't injured. The ICU nurses went on with their work, watching but letting the drama pass. I ducked my head, feigned interest in the chart, and smiled to myself.

Darren's voice came softly. "Carlos, it's all right now. He's gone. It's all right, baby."

Carlos seemed to regain control of himself and embraced his partner. "That asshole has no right."

"I know. It's all over. It's all right. He ran off."

"No right to be here, not at a time like this."

"I know. It's finished. He's gone."

"No right."

"I know. It's over." Darren relaxed his embrace and smiled. "I think you scared the shit out of him. He probably didn't know if you were going to fuck him up or just fuck him."

The two started to chuckle, then laugh and cry. After many minutes, they wiped away each other's tears and began to settle.

"I love you." Carlos spoke gently.

"I love you too, even if you are a psycho."

I swallowed hard and looked up. Amidst the swaying pines, I could hear the cubs' growls as they kept climbing. I tilted my head, trying to see, and made out two furry forms at the top of a monstrous conifer. Man, I thought, anything that can climb like that has a chance. They definitely have a chance to survive, no matter what the odds, no matter what the obstacles.

For a long while, I stood motionless, listening. I wanted to hear something, some stirring on the wind, something faint or profound. Or maybe what I hoped for was just some sign of forgiveness. A strong gust blew up the gorge, eliciting more growls, but the cubs clung to the tree. Maybe, if they stay together—

I looked down and kicked the dirt. It must have been an anthill, because a few ants ran from the disruption, while others scurried to repair the damage. From overhead, a hawk issued a shrill cry, and I looked upward but could not see the bird. I turned away, and with a very real sadness realized I would just never know.

PART TWO

CHAPTER NINE

Being Invincible

Ursula

"My belly hurts so bad." I was only seven years old, holding my belly as I sat in class alongside my friend Prakashni. I asked permission to visit the washroom, but the loo gave no relief. Eventually, Mrs. Naidoo dismissed me, and after I struggled home, my mother sent me directly to bed. I fell asleep, yet two hours later when I awoke I could scarcely walk, and the pain had migrated to my right side.

With no transportation, my mother sent my sister Beverly to Dr. Arnanth's office. He came to our house within the hour, and after a brief examination announced that I probably had appendicitis and needed to go immediately to hospital.

To hospital, to hospital! My mind raced with excitement at the prospect of going to a modern, high-tech hospital, meeting other patients, rubbing elbows with doctors and nurses. A child's view, unrealistic, but mine even so. I couldn't articulate my thoughts, but trusted that the hospital would both provide the necessary cure and somehow initiate me into the world of adults.

Unable to reach my father, my mother got "Uncle" Mathew to come in his place. In the Indian community, family friends were typically referred to as "auntie" or "uncle." Now, Uncle Mathew, a co-worker of my father's, was Caucasian, British to be specific, and blond. He visited us often and seemed unmindful of the fact that he was not of Indian stock.

He stood in our living room in his work overalls, looking somber, as he and my mother discussed the situation, and soon he was driving us to the hospital. Every bump in the road along the way caused my belly to hurt, and by the time we reached our destination I was crying, in horrendous pain. Uncle Mathew lifted me out of the car and carried me to the hospital's reception area where, feeling safe in his arms, I closed my eyes. Even when they whisked me away on a gurney a few moments later, rolling me toward a drug-induced sleep, I kept my eyes closed and smiled, certain that I would soon know the hospital and this new, sophisticated world.

To my right, a child was wailing, but I felt groggy, drifting in and out of slumber. I squeezed my eyes shut against some harsh light. The child's cry gathered pitch and volume, then I heard a man's solicitous voice. "Almost finished, almost finished, young man. No need to cry. Your body's making an excellent job of it."

By and by the boy's cries subsided, I heard the man leave the room, and I managed to open my eyes to see, in the next bed, what seemed to be a mummy. He was wrapped in gauze from head to toe, and my curiosity overcame politeness.

"What happened to you?"

He turned, his eyes peeking out from the bandages.

"My auntie's house caught fire, and it caught me too."

"Are you burnt everywhere?"

"The doctor says fifty or sixty percent of my body. All I know is, it hurts when they change the bandages or bathe me."

With that I remembered my manners. "I'm Ursula. What's your name?"

"Rakesh. Pleased to meet you, Ursula. What brings you to hospital?."

"Appendicitis, I believe." I touched the edge of my bandage, feeling rather proud of it and at the same time irresistibly sleepy. "I'm sorry, Rakesh." My eyes closed, and I slept for some time, then awoke crying.

"Everything is all right, Ursula." The nurse seemed cross. "No need to cry."

I tried to hold still, but a needle seemed to be poking my side. "But, ma'am, my belly hurts."

"It will for quite some time. Doctor Dariwal said your appendix had nearly burst, but everthing is fine now."

"But it hurts!"

"I can give you a bit more pain medicine, Ursula, but we simply cannot stop all the pain. Right now, you need to be a brave little girl." She patted my shoulder and casually turned away.

I grimaced, feeling tears well in my eyes, and looked toward the next bed. "Rakesh? Rakesh?"

"No need to trouble yourself. He'll be back." The nurse's face reappeared, less cross. "He's gone to physiotherapy, been in hospital a month already, and he goes five times a week. Oh my, that child has, quite frankly, had a time of it. He endures, endures, endures." She sighed, shaking her head.

I didn't know what to say.

She smiled at me. "Do you need more pain medicine?"

I nodded, and she injected some medicine into the tube in my arm before leaving to tend to other patients. Soon the stab in my side diminished a bit. I closed my eyes, but I remained awake and keenly aware. I knew that I was in hospital, that my appendix had been removed, and that I would recover in due course. No longer excited or eager, I now felt strangely small, alone, and rather less than brave.

Clint

The nurse at Station #3 in the family care center glanced down the hallway and lost her smile. Like a gunslinger coming into town to start trouble, Betsy Rangel was shuffling into clinic. She hated waiting and wasn't bashful about letting it be known. Her tongue was sharp, her no-nonsense eyes like razors, and attempts to placate her got nowhere at all.

Betsy had heart failure ("the pump's wore out"), atrial fibrillation ("the ticker ain't a tickin' "), diabetes ("sugar"), and a lower back that "hurt like the devil." Beyond all that, she had myelodysplasia, a bone disorder that caused anemia and required frequent blood transfusions.

Even though Betsy had quit smoking ten years before, she remained a portrait of an aged Marlboro woman. Her face was wrinkled, white leather, thanks to her long-standing, squint-eyed defiance of the Texan sun. Faint traces of red in her gray-white hair suggested her younger locks matched her fiery temper. Often she leaned forward, frowning, and turned her right ear toward the speaker, but she almost never wore her hearing aide.

Suspicious of people who said they wanted to help her, Betsy was particularly unhappy with Stacey, a competent, soft-spoken, African-American nurse. At first, I attributed her attitude to racism, given Betsy's country accent and skin color, but later I learned that the prejudice was all my own. At the age of fifty-three Betsy had adopted Drew, a five-year-old foster child from Nigeria and had loved him tenaciously into adulthood. She often announced his accomplishments and attributes to anyone who would listen.

Seeing me always sparked Betsy's smile. Once I got to know her, I learned to come in, sit, and just listen for five or ten minutes. I knew I held no cure, no magic medicine to wipe away her ailments and rewind her life. With other patients, I sometimes felt pressed to prescribe, advise, and evaluate, while Betsy got from me the only thing she seemed to want – to be heard.

"Dr. Pearson, I hope you gonna talk to that girl in the hallway. She's so drunk she's a laughin' and fallin' down, and I can't much stand to see it. Such a young and perty girl, and she ain't got no idea what she's a doin.' Breaks my heart some'n fierce.

"I ain't being no holier-than-thou preacher. I know how it is. When we was young, me and my husband Ansel – God rest his soul – we used to carry on, and sometimes, late at night, them Schnapps and shots would taste mighty good. And let me tell you, Ansel could laugh with the best of 'em.

"But we was no more'n dumb kids, and it got Ansel. He couldn't get away from it, couldn't let it go. But you got to stop some time, 'cause sooner or later there ain't nothing to laugh at.

"Now, Ansel, he tried to quit. Lord knows he tried, and I knowed he loved me and the kids more'n anything, but it plumb twisted him and made him hate. When he was in the bar, he hated the world, wanted to fight ever'one for no good reason, but when he was home, it was worse. He hated hisself.

"He was a good man, and I loved him plenty, even when we weren't a laughin', but when I see a young person like that girl, staggerin' 'round and actin' like she got no sense, well, I can't much stand it."

It was a spring day when Betsy showed up with a kidney infection. While her sweaty face was contorted in pain, her eyes remained focused and firm. Through clenched teeth she reported severe back pain, burning with urination, and feet that were "swoll up like marshmallows."

With the approval of an attending physician, I admitted her to the hospital, but during the night Betsy's heart began to falter under the dual strain of anemia and fever. Her lungs began to fill with fluid, and she panted, in and out of consciousness.

The next morning I found that on-call staff had moved her to the ICU, where I read about the night's drama in her chart. Yet charts never tell the entire story — the shifting, slippery battle between life and death, dark and light, the fight to stay awake, the struggle to breathe, and the fear of loss that brings both terror and exhilaration. And sometimes when the battle is won, it's actually lost.

"I was in Heaven, just a floatin' on light like a bird. Oh, Dr. Pearson, it was real beautiful, and I was happy 'cause there ain't nobody hurtin' or being mean up there. There was music, but it seemed quiet 'cause the music was really colors. I can't much 'splain it, I can't." Betsy shook her head, smiling. "And time's different; it's kinda like a kid's kite string, all tangled up. Things in the past ain't really in the past; they ain't someplace else, no sir. If you're a thinkin' 'bout something, you're a thinkin' 'bout it now."

Betsy eyes followed the clear tubing from her arm to the I.V. pole. "But I ain't much good at 'splainin' it, and — " She sucked air, grimaced, tried to shift position. "It was plumb different, and I sure didn't want to come back, no sir, no reason to."

"Well, Betsy, I know I'm not much to look at, but that's no reason to want to die."

"Oh, Dr. Pearson, don't make me laugh." She smiled over clenched teeth. "I'm old and I'm tard, and I ain't never seen things as good as that."

"Well, I'm glad you're back. Some of us wouldn't mind keeping you around a little longer."

"But I can't catch my breath, and it feels like someone's got a cattle prod on my backside."

"Where? Your lower back?"

"Yes sir, down low and deep, it's a-achin' somepn fierce." She clenched her jaw and shook her head. "Dr. Pearson, I want to go back. Why am I here?"

"I guess it just wasn't your time, Betsy."

"Why wasn't it?" Her eyes were soft and wet, pleading for an answer.

"I don't know." My honesty brought several moments of silence.

"Well, at least, now I know where I'm a-going, and there ain't no pitchforks and fire, but I ain't never had pain like this."

"Don't worry. I'll change you to a stronger pain medicine." I patted her hand, and she raised her head and offered a crooked smile.

Within twelve hours, Betsy's congestive heart failure improved. The medicines drove the fluid from her lungs, and her breathing fell into a soft, unconscious rhythm. I moved her from the ICU to the medical floor where Betsy was no longer awakened every hour, no longer smothered with an oxygen mask, wasn't poked and prodded with needles and inane questions. On the other hand, she was seldom checked on, talked to, or cleaned up, even when her bladder spilled urine onto the sheets.

I saw her the next morning and was immediately alarmed. Dawn's light was slanting between the blinds and across Betsy's face in a distorted pattern.

"Oh, Dr. Pearson, I hurt so bad, and these here nurses

won't help me atall. I told 'em to call you last night, but they wouldn't, and they won't clean me up. I'm in so much pain, I ain't got no control." She glanced downward and tried to swallow.

"Betsy, it's okay. Did you wet yourself?"

"I'm real sorry I did, but the nurses don't much care. They're mean as copperheads, and that fuzzy-haired one won't come in no matter how much I press the button."

"Let's back up. Your back hurts really bad, and you can't control your urine. Is that right?"

"Yeah, and I can't sleep, and the nurses don't care."

"Hold on. Let's clean you up and then we'll talk about what to do with your back."

I found the night nurse, who was surprised to find Betsy's bed wet. After a rapid and skillful bedding change, she spoke to me outside the room. Named Sasha, she was clearly exhausted, telling me that the higher-ups imagined her job to be little more than watching over sleeping patients, merely a safeguard in case someone just happened to wake up in the middle of the night and need a drink of water.

In reality, Sasha had ten patients to care for, ten patients needing position changes every two hours, ten patients needing vital signs taken every four hours, eight patients with Alzheimer's dementia, two patients soiling the bed, five wetting the bed, and three of those wetting the bed twice. Two patients wanted pain pills, four wanted sleeping pills, and one couldn't be awakened. One patient wanted to talk to the doctor, one wanted to talk to his dead wife, and all the while, buzzers sounded and panel lights flashed until Sasha disappeared into the bathroom to collapse, sobbing, on the cold tile floor.

"It's all right. I understand. You can't do everything. You did your best. Go home and get some sleep." After I gave her a hug and a pat on the back, she wiped away tears to manage a shaky smile.

"Maybe I'm just tired." She shook her head and started to walk away.

"Oh, one thing before you go," I called after her. She stopped, turned back.

"Could you get me a cup of coffee and rub my shoulders?" I feigned shoulder tightness and tried unsuccessfully to keep a straight face.

"You bastard," she whispered through a wry smile.

When I strode back into Betsy's room, she was ready for me.

"That there nurse don't care."

"She cares, Betsy, but she needs a lot more help. There was only one of her, and she couldn't do it all. But let's figure out what's going on with your back."

"My back hurts so bad. Oh Lord, it ain't never hurt so bad."

I was already pressing on her back, feeling the muscles, the tightness. An attempt to lift her leg elicited a shriek of pain, followed by moans of "my back, my back, my back!" I banged on her knees with my stethoscope but got no response.

"Betsy, you may have a bad back problem called spinal stenosis, and the way to find out is to do a special test called a CT myelogram."

"Oh, Dr. Pearson, I can't take this here pain. I'm old and wore out. I'm ready to go. There ain't nothing more for me to do."

"Well, somebody has to make me work for a living, and you do that better than most." I smiled, but Betsy didn't. "I tell you what, until we get this special test on your back, I'll give you a stronger pain medicine, one that comes in a patch, and another medicine to help you sleep. We'll get things squared away, no problem."

I discussed Betsy's case with the attending physician, then ordered a CT myelogram, a Fentanyl patch, and a sleeping pill. Satisfied with my clinical competence, I felt confident that Betsy's problems could be solved.

The CT myelogram confirmed spinal stenosis with nerve impingement. Betsy's degenerating spine was crushing her spinal cord and the nerve roots that come off it. Yet the treatment was surgery, and given Betsy's medical problems, I doubted that any neurosurgeon would consider it. The surgical risks were simply too great. There was too great a chance that Betsy would die facedown on the operating table.

Even so, I phoned a neurosurgeon in a nearby city, although I never mentioned the conversation to anyone.

"Dr. Wilson, I've got a seventy-two-year-old female with lumbar spinal stenosis, and she needs an operation, but she has some serious medical problems."

"Okay, what's she got?"

"Hypertension."

"Okay."

"Insulin-dependent diabetes, type two

"Yeah, go on."

"Myelodysplasia requiring progressively frequent blood transfusions."

"Well—"

"Atrial fibrillation with intermittent rapid ventricular response, coronary artery disease, and congestive heart failure with a recent exacerbation."

"Hold it. Stop a second. Now you're one of the residents there, right? Not a lot of experience with neurosurgical cases?

"Well, yeah."

"The bottom line is this. This woman is not a surgical candidate. If she survived surgery, and she probably wouldn't, she'd never make it through rehab."

"I understand. I suspected as much, but I wanted to check to be sure. Thanks for your time." I replaced the telephone, shaking my head and muttering to myself.

The attending physician asked, "Are you ready to send Betsy to a nursing home?"

I exhaled and looked up. "I can't see any alternative other than sending her to a nursing home and trying to control her pain."

"You realize that sending a patient to a nursing home is usually the first nail in the coffin, so to speak?"

"Yeah, but what else can we do?"

"Well, we could get one of the anesthesiologists to try epidural steroids. It may not work, but if it did, it might keep her out of a nursing facility for a while."

Falling

"Sounds great." My spirits revived.

Like a stage magician preparing his props, the anesthesiologist came to Betsy's bedside and arranged an assortment of plastic coverings, sterile swabs, and medications. He had Betsy turn onto her side, then after loading a syringe with a clear fluid, he attached a needle and stabbed it between two vertebrae. The effect was soon evident.

"My back don't hurt. At least, not like it did. Thank you, Dr. Pearson, I knew you'd fix me up. Thank you."

With mock indignation, the needle-wielder said, "Hey, I'm the guy who gave you the shot."

"Thank you, too." Betsy shifted in bed, this time without wincing.

"Now you can't go dancing yet. Lie in bed and take it easy. Hopefully, this shot will last a while." He was already packing some of his props, tossing discarded materials in the nearby trashcan.

Betsy's face was drained, crumpled and pale, her white sweaty hair wildly rumpled, but her smile seemed to belong to someone much younger. I smiled back as the anesthesiologist and the rest of the team left the room.

"Dr. Pearson, it's better, but I don't never want to feel pain like that again." Betsy shook her head as a single tear rolled down her wrinkled cheek. When I offered a box of tissues she took one but just rolled it between her fingers.

I patted her hand, hoping to control my emotions. "Betsy, I don't want you to hurt like that again. With luck, that epidural will last a month or so, then maybe we can give you another one. We also need to give you a blood transfusion. I know it's only been two weeks, but you need one."

"But why am I needin' it so soon?"

"I don't know, but your blood level's been dropping faster in recent months, and it'll put a strain on your heart if we don't stay ahead of it."

"That's fine. A transfusion ain't no big deal, but I don't want to hurt like that." She started to get emotional again, then pulled herself together in another smile.

"How's your family doing with this recent turn of events?"

"Fred and Samantha are gonna be up here today, but Drew don't know I'm sick. He's off at college, and I don't want him to worry none or go and leave school for no good reason."

"You might consider telling him. He'll probably want to be here or, at least give you a call."

"Oh, he calls most ever' weekend, and I figure I'll be home by Saturday, long as my back don't act up again." Betsy pressed a button to raise the head of her bed a little. "But, Dr. Pearson, you look wore out. I know'd for some time now that you got that nerve disease."

"Multiple sclerosis."

"Yeah, that one. How you been a-doin' with it?"

"Me?" I'd been seeing a local neurologist, and since one of the perks of my residency was health insurance, I was considering one of the new MS treatments—Avonex, Copaxone, Betaseon – something other than prednisone. Yet at best the treatments could only slow the progression, not improve my function. And then there were side effects. I grinned at her. "Don't worry about me, Betsy. I'm invincible."

"Now, you ain't no Superman. You need your rest and—"

"Betsy, it's okay, really. I'm okay." I shook my head. "With luck, that epidural will last a while. Just keep your fingers crossed."

"I will. Don't you worry none 'bout me."

"Okay, take care, and I'll see you tomorrow."

I smiled, shuffling toward the door and my other patients. As I headed out, I heard a voice, "I'll be here."

At the nurse's station, I wrote an order in Betsy's chart for a blood transfusion. With a blood level lower than ever, she'd probably need another transfusion tomorrow. I tried not to think about the long-term implications. Resources were limited, and with no end in sight, no light at the end of the tunnel, I had few hopes of saving Betsy to see Drew's graduation.

"Shit."

"What's up with you, Dr. Pearson? Somebody steal your

stethoscope?" Patricia, Elsie, and some of the other nurses were laughing, having fun with the doctor who had fun with them.

"Sorry, I was just thinking. I bet none of you would be willing to give Betsy Rangel your heart for a heart transplant."

"A heart transplant? You must be crazy."

"And you call yourselves nurses. "

"Well, if we don't do it, are you going to give Betsy your heart?"

"You must be kidding. I'm a doctor. I'm very important. Nurses, well, what can you say? They're a dime a dozen."

"Ooo, we're going to have to beat you up." Patricia and Elsie put up their dukes.

"Never mind, never mind." I started walking away, adding under my breath, "You probably don't have hearts anyway."

Although I couldn't walk fast, the nurses were giggling too much to pursue. "We heard that. We got plans for you when you come back."

Sometimes the most carefully made plans are just wasted effort, a self-deluded attempt to control the future and ward off disaster. Sometimes the magician stumbles, the magic evaporates, and the trick fails.

"The pain's worse than ever." Betsy's eyes looked wild.

"When did it start?"

"Last night, it started hurtin' some – I did my best to ignore it – but it got worse and worse."

"Do you have the pain patch on?"

"Yeah, it's on, but it ain't doin' much. Oh, I want to die, it hurts so bad." Several tears rolled down Betsy's weathered face.

"I'm going to order some shots in the I.V., and we'll get your pain under control, but, Betsy, I don't want to lie to you. If the epidural's already worn off, it's a bad sign."

I didn't want to say what I had to say next. "Betsy, I don't think you're going to be able to go home. You're going to need nursing care to control your pain and help you."

I waited for a response, but Betsy just stared out the

window and twisted a tissue between her fingers.

"Betsy? Betsy?"

She turned slowly. "I wish I had a red ribbon for my hair. When I was a girl, I had one, and right now my hair's a-goin' ever'where." She looked back toward the window. "And why don't they get some more trees 'round here?"

"We'll see if we can get something for your hair, but, Betsy, we need to talk about the nursing home."

"I don't want to go to no nursin' home. I only want to die and go back to Heaven." She was looking out the window, seemed to be talking to herself.

"Well, some nursing homes aren't that bad. They'll look after you, and your family can visit all the time. And they'll give you pain medicine so you can sleep and feel better."

"I'll think 'bout it, but right now I'm hurtin' too bad."

"Let me tell the nurse to get you a big dose of Demerol. You'll probably go to sleep, but then you can think about it." I waved and shuffled toward the door. I couldn't bring myself to say that she didn't have much of a choice.

The Demerol did its job. It let Betsy sleep, and Betsy's face relaxed as she snored. When she half-awoke two hours later, she called out for her mother. The nurse heard her, reassured her, and soon Betsy drifted back asleep. Within twenty minutes, however, Betsy awoke fully and asked to see her doctor. I arrived an hour later, feeling tired, and limped into her room.

"I'll go to a nursin' home, but I want 'em to handle this damn pain and help me sleep, and I don't want to take no more pills. I can't swallow 'em, and I only want to die. I don't mind gettin' a transfusion, but I ain't gonna be goin' back and forth, hurtin' my back. I don't need no more transfusions after today. And nobody better be mean to me, or so help me—" Her voice trailed off.

She looked determined – jaw fixed, eyes steady. The gunslinger had returned, and although she knew she couldn't win this last gunfight, she was determined not to grovel in the dust or prolong the inevitable.

"It's okay, Betsy. I won't do anything you don't want me

to do."

I wasn't sad, not even a little, just relieved. "I'm sorry I can't do more for you, but we will control your pain, now and when you're in the nursing home."

"I know you'll do all you can, and I want you to be my doctor till the end, but I know you can only do so much." She smiled. "When will I be going to the nursin' home?"

"Maybe tomorrow, if I can arrange it. You'll have another doctor over there, but I'll still be seeing you as well."

"Two doctors. I hope I can tell you apart." She displayed a smile that became a grimace.

"I'll tell the nurse to get you some Demerol."

I felt a lightness as I gave the order, but before I could enjoy the release of tension, before I could breathe deeply and sit down, stretch my legs and tease the nurses again, my beeper sounded, summoning me STAT to the labor and delivery ward. I walked as fast as I could and worried about what might await me, but on my way there I couldn't forget the girlish gunfighter who faced death open-eyed and wanted a red ribbon for her hair.

Nursing homes aren't as bad as people think. The residents are generally not forgotten or completely ignored. Nobody is shoved into a closet and starved, but the ambience can be disturbing. Elderly women with bent backs babble to invisible friends; toothless, smelly guys putter along in their wheelchairs and try to convey some urgent, unfathomable point to anyone who'll listen; and schizophrenics smack their lips and thrust their tongues, their shirt fronts decorated with scrambled eggs, strawberry jam, or some other unidentifiable food.

Families are often shocked and sad to see the deterioration of their grandmothers, grandfathers, great-aunts, or parents. The nurses and nurses' aides tend to complain or hide. Some surreptitiously smoke in the bathroom, others gossip or sigh or speak nonstop about other jobs. Even when it's quiet, those other jobs are always near, more alluring work with better pay, better hours, fewer hassles, and less soiled bedding.

Sometimes when I visited Betsy in the nursing home she

was awake and eager to talk about her life, but at other times, she slept and I had to settle for speaking with her daughter and son-in-law. To them, I explained the medicines, much of which Betsy refused, outlined the pain-control plan, and spoke somberly of Betsy's refusal to eat even small amounts of food.

Yet despite my effort to appear knowledgeable, I adjusted Betsy's pain medicines clumsily, inexperienced resident that I was. I stopped the Demerol when the needles made Betsy's butt too tender, only to discover that the fentanyl patch and Lortab couldn't do the job without it. At the same time, I came to see that some nurses, concerned about the potential for addiction, were withholding her pain medicines, at least, any designated "as needed."

Eventually, I made sure Betsy got all her pain medicines, but my failure to use long-acting pain-killers, except for the fentanyl patch, meant that Betsy's pain fluctuated too much, and she never reached the continuous, sleepy, low-pain state found in hospice textbooks.

Yet even when the pain was controlled, Betsy was increasingly demanding, wanting to know why she wasn't in Heaven yet, tortured by her memory of Heaven but not able to visit again. Like a convict chained to a post, she remained rooted in her rotting body, slowly starving, skin sagging and eyes sunken. Her muscles soon withered, no longer able to perform even simple movements.

Before long, only memories remained of a girl growing up in northern Texas, memories of climbing trees in the city park, of laughing atop a tall cottonwood and defying the wind. Sometimes she was playing in the rain on the Fourth of July or skinny-dipping in Lake Texoma. Sometimes she was dancing with look-away boys, and her hips were swinging, teasing, but touching rhythms far more playful than seductive.

Still the touches, the kisses, and the surrender came, even for a rock-tossing tomboy, even in the cramped backseat of a '42 Chevy Coupe, and even on a night so humid that it brought a plague of locusts and peel-sticky clothes.

"Then came them babies, and they growed into shoeless and muddy children just like that, even though Ansel went and got hisself killed in a bar fight, and I barely had 'nough to feed the little scoundrels. Oh, but they were happy as hoot owls. They'd run 'round makin' noise and screamin' at each other, and they peed off the back porch till it smelt somethin' awful. Then in a few years, here come those grandkids, all nine of 'em.

"I gotta tell you, though, sometimes they didn't seem real 'cause they was too clean. But I don't know. I reckon they did pick their noses and smear their shirts with chocolate, when they thought nobody was a-lookin'.

"But as time passed they was there less and less. All my kids moved to big cities, to chase them better jobs, and they took the grandkids with 'em. Soon the house was too quiet, downright lonesome, and I knew I needed to go find the children, even if it meant goin' down to Dallas or up to Tulsa or even, God forbid, California."

The light was fading as I drove to the nursing home, with stars starting to spangle the sky. I was sleepy from late clinics, late-night calls, and all-night deliveries. Fortunately, the route was familiar, the movements automatic, and soon I was limping into Betsy's room.

When I touched her shoulder and said her name, her eyes didn't open. My stethoscope went to her chest – faint rumblings but no heartbeat, mouth open but no breath. I touched her cheek, gazing at her strange stillness. After a last deep breath, I turned and walked to the nurse's station.

"Betsy Rangel has expired." The euphemism comforted me. She wasn't dead, only lapsed, like a library card or a driver's license.

The nurse gave a start. "What? I was just in there. I told the family she was the same. They're on their way in."

I waited for them, rehearsing in my mind what to say. Sooner than I wanted, Samantha and Fred, Betsy's daughter and son-in-law, arrived.

"I'm sorry," I said. "She's gone. I'm sorry."

"When?"

"Just now." Samantha hugged me, then let go and started to cry. An actor who'd forgotten his lines, I stuck on "I'm sorry," unable to recall the rest. So we went to Betsy's room together, and for five minutes the two of them talked to Betsy in hushed tones, as if not wanting to wake her. All the while, I stood and stared, trying in vain to think about other things. When they were satisfied, they turned back to me, and I found some words.

"She was so strong. She battled through so much. At least now she can rest."

Tears streamed down Samantha's face, but she nodded and managed a smile before turning back to her mother.

"We'll be all right, Mom. I know you stayed with us as long as you could." Her voice quavered. "I love you." She leaned over and hugged the lifeless body. Her husband looked toward the ceiling, blinked, then looked at his shoes. Long moments of silence followed before I blurted it out again.

"I'm so sorry."

Betsy's daughter helped me. "Thanks for all your work and caring, Dr. Pearson. I know my mom is sometimes not the easiest person to take care of, but I know she appreciates what you did, and I want you to know we are real thankful for you." Her tears were drying, her face grave.

I looked back at the bed. "I'm sorry I couldn't do more, but it was a privilege to take care of her." My gaze moved from Betsy to Samantha. "Are you going to be okay?"

"Oh yeah, I'm even a little relieved. I didn't want it to drag on too long and have her suffering. I'm more concerned about Drew. He's on his way up from L.A., and he'll be upset at not getting to see her again."

"I'll leave you two alone with her. If you have any problems, don't hesitate to call me. You've got my beeper number. Or if Drew has any questions, have him call me." I said my exit line, relieved that my part was over.

Outside the building a strong breeze was making a Chinese sumac next to the parking lot dance and sway. I leaned into the wind, wanting to howl like a wolf. I wanted to rip off my tie, rush home sprinting and screaming and cursing, anything to avoid the stuffy rooms, anything to escape the strained faces that waited quietly, accusing with their stares.

A few minutes later when Ursula came to the door to greet me, I remained outside, leaning against the apartment's wall.

"Betsy Rangel has passed away."

"Oh, shame. Does the family know?"

"Yeah, I just saw them."

"Are they maintaining some semblance of sanity?"

"I guess so. They seem to be."

"Well, it was expected—" Her words faded, and she studied me for several moments. "I am sorry, but I'm certain everything will work out. Come inside." She stepped back, smiling. "I have prepared curry, rice, and dhal."

So I entered the apartment and tried to reestablish my life among the living. I ate a delicious dinner, enjoyed lively conversation, and then made love to my wife, but afterwards, as my body lay naked and exposed on the bed, my thoughts returned to the nursing home.

"I should have given her a morphine pump. She might have stayed asleep or even died sooner, but she wouldn't have ever hurt."

"Are you speaking of Betsy? Some people cuddle or smoke after intercourse, but you, you wish to discuss the subtleties of your job."

"Yeah, I know, but the morphine pump would have been better."

"It is finished now. There's absolutely no reason to concern yourself with the past. Simply go to sleep, you silly man." She snuggled against me, and I closed my eyes.

Soon I was dreaming, playing chess with only pawns and trying to catch a red ribbon that floated away. It swirled and settled into a tall tree, its bright red hue standing out against the green leaves and wafting, falling gently in the wind beyond my reach. Then I was building something, hammering nails on a hot, sunny day when suddenly, the pounding became gunfire, and I ran from the bullets screaming.

Then I half-woke, went back to sleep, and found myself climbing to the top of a tall, jagged peak. The view was spectacular, but a hot wind gusted, knocking me off. I looked down, expecting to see the ground rocketing toward me, but in the next moment I was flying, soaring on the air currents and playing with the birds. I started laughing then, at the absurdity, at the absolute folly of flying and being, and as I listened to my own childish glee, I could hear something beyond the laughter, past the squeal, something sage and strong and solid, and, yet, like a whisper in the wind, it was breathy and light and just elusive enough to be invincible.

CHAPTER TEN

Side Effects

Ursula

One evening when Clint came to fetch me at the end of my shift – I was working at a shelter for battered women – I noticed that he was rather quiet. He had planned to start a new MS medicine, Betaseron, on the weekend, and we had discussed the potential side effects – fever, fatigue, muscle pain. Yet Clint had not waited for the weekend and had injected the drug a couple hours before he came for me.

He complained of feeling chilled and began to shiver, and before we had traveled three or four blocks, he stopped the car and wanted me to drive. By the time he was in the passenger seat, he was shaking violently and crumpled into a fetal position. I secured his seatbelt, asking repeatedly what I must do – call 911, go to hospital, go to clinic?

Clint squirmed in his seat and blinked several times, as if not fully awake. He seemed in no hurry to respond to my questions, then slowly his eyes began to focus and he shrugged as if the answer was plain. "Drive us home."

Yet at home, still in our parking space, the answers were no longer obvious, even for Clint. He was able to speak but had fever and could not walk or even stand. So I did the only sensible thing – I called for assistance.

Within ten minutes, Jed and Katie Gray arrived and carried Clint inside our flat – Jed was a resident physician with Clint, and his wife Katie was my close confidant. We engaged the flat's cooling system, gave Clint some Motrin with an iced soft drink, and within minutes, he seemed as perfectly normal as a person with MS could be.

Unfortunately, throughout residency, Clint's MS progressed at an alarming rate. His walking became more and more of a lurch and limp, especially during our sweltering summer months. He increased his prednisone, started on Copaxone as well as Betaseron, added baclofen, and still the disease progressed. He saw two different neurologists, had two MRI scans, but nothing changed. He tried such over-the-counter products as vitamins, DHEA, herbs, and even an electrical device that, according to Clint, showed some value in one reputable study. But at the end of day, nothing helped.

Yet neither Clint nor I was overly preoccupied with his health. As often as possible, we filled our leisure time with conversation, laughter, and foods ranging from crab-stuffed ravioli to home-cooked chicken curry.

And when time permitted, we went to the cinema, three times, in fact, for Titanic. Each time, I watched my macho, mountain-climbing husband's heart melt. Each time, he had to stay in his seat after the movie ended, after the song and the credits, after the lights came on — ten or fifteen minutes after the rest of the audience was gone.

There we sat, the only two left, waiting in silence and staring at a blank screen, while Clint pretended he had a speck in his eye or lint on his glasses. The third time was part and parcel of the first, so I simply sat waiting, smiling at my emotional husband, a little embarrassed but still longing to touch him and hold him in ways not proper or even legal in a public movie theater.

Clint

Blood squirted from my thigh, and I dropped the syringe to clasp it.

"Ursh, come quick! I must have hit a vessel."

I felt fire climbing up my body to my face. It carried hot

bile to the back of my throat, but I swallowed it down, shaking my head. Ursh was there. When did she come through the door? She was panicked, her mouth open, making noise. I waved her away. How could I possibly deal with her problems and mine too? Oh, shit, the fire was trying to come out the other end.

I scrambled to the toilet and made it, barely.

Then the fire was burning my nose and eyes, in my throat again, making me belch. I waved ineffectually at the shower. Ursh understood and turned it on. Bless you, Ursh. I'll handle your problems after the shower, after the fire's out. I promise.

Ursh helped me up, grimacing. Damn, I must stink. Okay, just let me take a shower.

I was suddenly in the shower, in the cool water. The fire was no longer on my face, just inside. I swallowed some water, but it didn't help. My outside was cool, but the inside stayed hot, way too hot. Then my body was burning everywhere, flaming, flaring, even on the outside. Close the door Ursh, you'll get water on the floor. I need all the water to put out the fire, no wasting. Why is she looking at me like that? Just let me take a shower. Can't a guy take shower these days?

I'm just tired. That's it, just tired. Why am I standing? I need to save my energy. It takes a lot of energy to fight a fire. I need to move down, slowly, slow-motion like the six-million-dollar man. I'm tired, I need to rest, to sleep. Too much noise, though, pounding and screaming. Turn it off, Ursh, turn it off, please.

That's better. Did I turn it off with my mind? I must be psychic. Or was it Ursh? Quiet, except for the dripping. Floor's too hard, though. Tomorrow I need to remember, remember, remember, to put a pillow in here.

Wouldn't you know it? Here comes the fire again. Can't run, just fan the flames. Forget it. I don't want more water, too loud. What does Ursh want now? Fuck it. I can't deal with any of it now. She doesn't make sense. Blah, blah, blah. I'm going to sleep. I'll help Ursh with her problems in the morning. Tomorrow — in the morning — deal with it then — in the morning . . .

"Clint. Clint. Can you hear me?"

Jed, what are you doing here? I'm trying to sleep, but the floor's too hard. I got to remember to put a pillow in here. Remember, remember, pillow, pillow.

"I'm going to pull you out."

All I need's a pillow, but since you're already pulling — Man, watch the rail, that's rough on my butt — Now that's soft, very soft but still no pillow.

Damn, this is a bad idea. The carpet's way hotter than the shower. Here comes the fire again. Maybe, if I'm still and go to sleep, it won't find me. Still, still, don't breathe. Crap, too late, I'm burning up. I need ice, ice water. No! No! I need to get back in the shower. Oh shit, it's too far. I can't make it, can't breathe. The fire must be stealing my oxygen. I need air now, fast, fast. "Call 9-1-1."

Lights red when eyes close and breathing hot. Fire in my mouth, in my belly, bubbling out flowing fizz-slow thick like lava but my eyes shut see red just red, see fire, are fire now. Now floor is fire, lapping trickling burning on my back neck face eyes throat, furnace-hot boiling blowing. Loud blasts booming turbines screaming screeching, my head deep down flushing full sizzle.

Drop and roll, drop and roll. Let it go, go go, just let it go. Be still, be still, Find it, find something good, soothing good water. Bumblebee sting-hurt stuck sticky legs on my arm but buzz, buzz away, gone now. Now floor rocking rising floating above flames into dark cool-wind shiver quiet — fluttering away from fire-choke and humming softly, space empty. Just sleep now just sleep — sleep . . .

Lights, fluorescent and moving like railroad tracks, whisking by, but place is active, familiar. What train am I on?

"Trauma room two."

I thought I finished my shift at the hospital. What's on my arm?

"What's the story?"

"Thirty-three-year-old male, Dr. Pearson, presents with nausea, diarrhea, and fever of 105.9 after injecting a multiple-sclerosis medicine called—"

"I'm burning up." Man, these lights are bright, and I can't fucking breathe.

"Doctor Pearson, how are you feeling?" Dr. Ramirez looked tired.

"Very hot. Gotta get this fever down – fast. I – can't – handle – fevers – this –high – can't breathe."

"First, tell me what happened."

"No, no time to talk. Ramirez. Pack me in ice." I could feel cotton-dry drool tumbling from my mouth, but I couldn't move to wipe, could only spit it out with my words.

"It's all right. You injected your medicine and then—"

"No! No time! Pack me in ice!" For a moment, I could see only crimson, and I coughed out what felt like dusty cobwebs, only they were hot.

"It's all right. We'll get your fever down. Nurse, get him six hundred milligrams of Motrin. Any allergies?"

"No, no, no. I can't take fever this high. Pack me in ice, damn it!"

"Just relax. It's all right."

"I am not delirious! Pack me in ice or get the fuck out of here!"

I knew my face was aflame. When I saw Ursh, she looked like she did when her father died. Then she looked at me like I was crazy, but I knew, I knew.

I was screaming, "Pack me in ice! Pack me in ice!" I screamed at a nurse, who glanced fearfully at Dr. Ramirez, but he just grimaced, mumbled, and walked away.

As he left, another nurse came in. "Here's the Motrin."

I swallowed the pill, with difficulty. I choked, and my throat felt seared, disconnected, filled with dry, hot spit. I had to keep coughing, spitting, just to breathe. Fuck, I'm losing my airway, drowning in heat and these people want to talk blah blah blah. Fuck you!

I was yelling again. "Pack me in ice, pack me in ice now!"

Everyone was staring at me. I could barely stand it. Wake up! Wake up, it's me.

"Pack me in ice!" The two nurses froze, wide-eyed, looking toward the doorway for help.

Suddenly I saw Jed. "Jed, get them to pack me in ice."

When he spoke it was with a Jimmy Stewart stammer. "Well, uh, well, I-I-I'm not actually working, you know."

"Then I'm working, damn it. Pack me in ice!"

Jed shrugged, looking worried and frustrated. The nurse left, and I looked at the ceiling at first then had to turn back, panting, gagging.

Ursh touched my face with trembling fingers.

"Ursh, are they getting ice?"

"I don't know, I don't know." Her voice cracked.

A nurse was back with an ear thermometer.

"Okay, let's see where we're at." I couldn't feel the thermometer, but I heard the beeps. "One oh five point four. You're hot."

Hell, yes, I'm hot. "Pack me in ice. Pack me in ice now!" More froth spilled onto my chin to bubble around my mouth, but I didn't care as long as I could breathe.

"Pack me in ice before you have to intubate me." Give the fucking order.

The nurse looked at Jed, who shrugged and turned palms up. Then she hurried out the door as quick and quiet as a burglar and came back a few seconds later with two plastic bags of ice.

"Open the bags! Put ice on my crotch, under my arms, then go get more."

She did it. I didn't feel the ice much – cool, maybe, definitely not cold.

After that I became calm, directing the ice burial and watching as my body vanished beneath the glassy chunks. The others in the room were grinning, chuckling and shaking their heads, tight-lipped and glancing around like children stealing chocolate cake. I breathed slowly in and out and shook my head, smiling. Ursh smiled.

In a few minutes, I felt the change, unseen and soundless but distinct.

"Okay, start to pull some of the ice away, slowly, no

rush. Leave the ice under my arms and on my belly and my groin but take it away from my legs and arms."

Apprehensive, Ursh asked, "Are you feeling better?"

"Yeah, I'm cooling. I'll be fine in a little bit. Ice is a wonderful invention."

"Okay, Doctor Iceman, let's check your temp." The nurse approached a little cautiously, as she would a sick drunk. The thermometer felt hard and cool.

"Better, one oh two point one."

I wiped my mouth. My right hand felt clumsy, like a piece of wood, but I could move. The hand fell back to my side, shifting some ice.

"I don't think I'm ready to do microneurosurgery, but I'm better."

Within a few minutes my body began to shiver.

"Okay, help me take off the rest of the ice. Then I'll sit up."

"You're not going anywhere. The attending is on his way, so just sit tight." The nurse looked irritated, annoyed at having to take orders from a patient, but she used a towel to clear away the rest of the ice.

Ursh had switched from anxiety to relief. "Clint, don't be difficult, not now. You need to simply wait. And I don't wish to hear any of that invincibility nonsense."

"Relax, I'm not going anywhere. I just want to sit up to stretch my lower back."

With Jed on one side and Ursh on the other, I rose up stiff and straight, bending at the waist like a vampire in a coffin. I knew I couldn't stand, but the worst was over.

I grinned, looking at Ursh. "One thing's for sure, we need to contact McNeil Pharmaceuticals right away."

"McNeil? Why do they deal with drug reactions?"

"No, they make Motrin. I'm sure it was the Motrin that cooled me down so fast and saved me. We need to buy some stock."

At first, Ursh just stared, squinting and scowling a little, her mouth half-open, as she tried to find the logic, but I couldn't hide my smile forever.

"Oh, might you be serious for once in your life?" Ursh tossed ice at me, and her lips pouted out her smile, sly and smoldering. "Next time you need to listen to me. Next time, quite possibly, I'll leave you in the shower. How might you like that?"

"That would be okay as long as you joined me or, at least, brought me a pillow."

CHAPTER ELEVEN

The Dying

Ursula

"How're we doing?" Clint was grinning, feigning interest, as I took stock of our numerous bills.

I had been ill and still didn't feel perky, not helped by our financial woes. I might also have felt resentment at being the only one responsible for or even remotely interested in our monetary situation. So when I answered, it was the truth.

"Not good at all."

For the first time, Clint seemed to take note. What he tallied – $25,112 in credit-card debt – shocked and angered him. He moaned, "You can't carry twenty percent interest. Oh my God, nobody can, not twenty percent." His face turned red, and he shook, gritted his teeth, and stomped up and down our hallway, ranting that we absolutely had to file for bankruptcy. He didn't curse at me but at everyone and everything else in this world

I wanted to explain that the debt had accumulated over ten years' time, that I had tried repeatedly to find a solution, but in the face of his anger I was at a complete loss for words. After putting my head in my hands, I simply wept and went on weeping for what seemed like days.

Clint

"Must you go? Why not stay here with me and chat a while? I'm quite certain we can find something to do." Like a model on a photo shoot, Ursula smiled and leaned against the wall outside our apartment's open door. In that pre-dawn hour, the porch light's glow provided the only illumination, throwing grotesque shadows on the wall and walkway.

"Come on, Creature." I looked toward the carport.

"Clint, hold it one moment. I am not a creature. My name is Ursula. Have you forgotten your wife's name?"

I smiled. "Look, I know you're the Creature, and you know you're the Creature. There's only one Creature. So embrace it, accept your creatureness."

Ursula rolled her eyes. "Please, do not avoid the subject. Why must you climb Dennison again? Tell me why? To prove you have testosterone on the brain?"

"It's just one weekend." I shrugged, looking away. "It's no big deal?"

"Why do we not do things that I wish to do?"

I set my backpack on the ground and walked to her, gently reaching for her hands. "What do you want to do? You can go with me if you like. I can get you on top of the Peak."

She pulled away. "I have no desire to climb Dennison. It's simply—" She frowned and sighed. "The MS is considerably worse, and you are not able to walk as before."

"Look, I've climbed Dennison Peak dozens of times. Have I ever gotten hurt? No. So just give me a break."

"Yes, but—"

"It just takes me longer. I know what I'm doing. Now just relax." I hugged her, gave her a kiss on her neck.

She squealed, pushing me away. "That tickles!" Then she gave a great sigh. "What more might I say? Will you be returning soon?"

"I'll be back forthwith or henceforth or with Godspeed. It just depends how drunk I get." I grinned, then did my best to appear sensible and calm. "I love you, Creature, don't worry. I'll be home Sunday."

"I love you, too."

I turned, picked up my backpack, and started for the car—no longer the old camouflaged Scout, now I had a Suzuki Samurai. It was about 4 a.m., quiet, with nobody else about in the apartment complex except for a scurrying cat. I struggled with the pack, got my gear loaded into the car, settled behind the wheel, and started the engine.

An hour and a half later, I headed toward a faintly glowing sky, the sky-lightening overture to sunrise. With an hour yet to go before I could put on my pack and start my climb, the distant outline of the mountains spurred me on.

Ten minutes later I stopped for gas at a mini-mart where the clerk sat putting sugar in his coffee.

"You going to the mountains or something?"

"Yep, ten dollars on number three."

"Said it might rain up there. Probably need a tent." He went on idly stirring, spilling coffee onto the countertop.

"Really? Well, I'm pretty waterproof."

"Always best to be prepared. What you need to— oh, crap, look what I've done."

I paid him and headed out. Another fucking Boy Scout. Sure, anybody could survive if they brought along a ton of gear. Camp stoves, tents, toothbrushes, pans, pads, lanterns, water purifiers, ropes – in other words, if they brought the city to the mountains. Why not just put a damn escalator up the side of Dennison?

Dawn had come when I turned right toward Yokohl Valley, and streaks of sunshine peeked over the mountains and brightened the twisting road. I could smell bear clover and put my foot down on the gas. Soon in sight of Dennison Peak, I drove even faster, hairpin turns and all, not slowing down until I'd sideswiped a roadside cluster of morning glories

"Hey, Pearson, don't be in a hurry to die." I repeated the admonition to myself, alive with anticipation. The Peak towered above me now, waiting.

When I stopped the car at an unmarked turnout and tried to step out, my legs shook in spasm. I scowled, waiting for them to relax. Too much goddamned sitting. In a few moments, the spasm passed, and after retying my boots and strapping on my pack I set off.

By mid-morning, I stood beside a stream, panting and swaying and checking my watch. On earlier climbs I'd made it to this spot in forty minutes, but today it had been more than three hours. I massaged my thighs, frowned, and heard Ursula's voice. You really should be careful. You are not able to walk as before.

I spat on some dry grass by the trail and considered the possibilities. I had only two days. What if I needed a third? Everyone will panic, especially the Creature. Search & Rescue will be called, put into action for nothing, and they'll probably stick me with the fucking bill.

An hour later my legs inexplicably loosened enough that I could increase my pace. Rests became rare, and soon I was climbing beneath a tall three-tiered waterfall toward a huge rock that marked the familiar route.

I tied the rope to my pack and gripped the other end between my teeth, then stretched up onto the rock. I wedged my hands into a crack, wriggled upward, and at the top, I pulled up my pack. Before I had time to wonder at my newfound vigor, I was marching up the draw faster than I'd walked in years.

In recent years rarely had my legs functioned so well. Trees, bushes, rocks, and waterfalls seemed to whiz by. The rhythm was automatic, exhilarating, and evoked scenes and feelings of days long past. The track-meet crowd was on its feet again, frenzied, shouting, and stomping the bleachers. Runners raced to the line, grunting and stretching toward the finishing tape.

As my body heated up, my breathing became labored. A lengthy rest, even a swim in the icy stream might have forestalled the muscle spasms, but the fever of the race, the memory, was too strong.

After climbing a steep bank I started across a ravine with a wide and shaky gait when my right foot landed on a wet rock. I felt it slide, felt the shock of pain as my ankle rolled. I fell, tumbling and sliding, and came to a stop on a mound of thick mud.

"Son of a bitch. Son of a bitch."

I grabbed my ankle to rock back and forth in the muck. With that my legs started to spasm, and I had to lie back and wait until the spasms stopped. When I was able to get up, I limped to a nearby boulder and sat down.

It took me thirty minutes to remove most of the mud and tape my ankle, but my first effort to walk made me grimace, and I sat back down to the sound of a familiar voice. Please be careful. Do not do anything silly. I simply do not understand why you wish to make me worry.

Relax. Just a little ankle sprain. It'll toughen up. No problem. Just keep pushing. Keep pushing.

Ten minutes later as the throbbing in my ankle began to subside, I set off again, following my usual path away from the creek. Soon the route came back to the stream, but before I could rest or drink, I stumbled, falling forcefully onto the rocks.

Shit, Pearson, stay on your feet. You do that on the Peak and you're dead. I shucked off my pack, opened it, pulled out a granola bar, and tore the paper off in wild frustration.

I don't care! I don't care! Legs, you're going up this mountain!

After a bite, I threw the opened granola bar back in my pack, crawled to the stream, and thrust my face into the water – so cold it made me pull back. "Maaaaan! Is that cold or what? Woooo, son of a bitch!"

The next time I dipped my head and sucked up the icy stuff more carefully. After a long drink, I rolled onto my back, shut my eyes, and allowed the sound of the gurgling brook to still my mind.

When I opened my eyes again and tried to get going, my legs were stiff. Keep going. You'll loosen up. Clearly this was to be a long-drawn-out competition, me against my MS.

After three hours, my stride hadn't changed, and the shadows were lengthening as I began to climb out of the gorge. Goddammit, this is supposed to be summer. I stopped, scowling at the sky, and unbuttoned my pants to pee. I stood, waiting, aware that it might be more than I could do to reach the top of the ridge before nightfall. Dammit, I don't have time for this crap. I looked down and pushed on the lower part of my belly. The wind gusted up the draw, rustling through the trees, and I pushed on my belly again.

Suddenly the humor struck me. Hey, I guess I'm just pissed off. Before long I managed to empty my bladder and looked up to smile at the sunset.

I pressed on up the mountain, grabbing bushes to steady myself, and Ursula's voice came back. There is simply no reason to do this, no reason to torture yourself.

I spat and rested, pulled out my water bottle and drank.

Soon I was back trudging up the hill, laboring, stumbling, falling now and then, but the night cooled my face and silenced that voice.

At the sight of a dark stump some thirty yards ahead, I halted, when all of a sudden it moved. I pulled out my Old Timer, but as soon as I did I knew it wasn't necessary. The bear was already running away and crashing through bushes.

"You better get out of here, bear!" I shouted the words and stood with chest puffed out, grimacing, gripping the knife. But I was running out of steam and I knew it. I let out my breath and slumped to the ground.

"Yeah, if you come over here, bear, I've got a knife, and I'll cut my own throat before you can eat me."

Soon I was up and moving again, and as the darkness deepened, as bushes and logs faded to black, as ground could be felt but not seen, and as stars began to pierce the night sky, I crested the ridge to stagger onto a level patch of ground that would be my campsite.

I barely managed to shed my pack before I crumpled to the ground. The night was clear and cool, and the wind starting to blow through the pines made an eerie sound.

I sat, staring at nothing, listening, feeling the coolness, thinking about patients, about fast bears and close races, finally about nothing. I untied my sleeping bag, took off my boots, and spread the bag on the ground. Soon I was snuggled in down, munching the rest of that granola bar and gazing at the sky. Then I was drifting with the wind into another world, more thoughts of running and racing, more memories of sweet sweat and freshly mowed grass. The tape stretched tense and waiting, and the flashbulbs all went off.

Raindrops were pattering on my face. Instantly awake, I slid on my boots without lacing them. The wind was shifting the shower here and there, like sea spray at the ocean's edge. I got up to carry my sleeping bag under a nearby pine. The pack could get wet, but I needed the bag dry.

Under the tree's protection I nestled into the bag again, but before I let myself fall asleep I watched for a bit, wary lest the night become intense and cold, sending me from dreams to shivers.

I woke in bright sunshine, squinting and scowling, and threw open my bag to cool down. When I sat up with a grunt and looked at my watch it was 9:42. The nighttime storm had gone, but the rain had permeated the air, leaving everything as stagnant and sticky as Tijuana.

But this was Dennison, not Mexico. And the air was not supposed to be hot and soggy, not even in July. I felt the change, smelled it – nothing to do but endure. Usually the stroll down the ridge was fast and bouncy, but my legs were sluggish, and my face seemed to burn. I stopped, reaching for my water bottle, but the liquid was warm both in my mouth and on my head. Then my right leg started to spasm, and I dropped to my knees to stretch. It's okay, you'll bounce back, no problem. I was lying to myself and I knew it.

I shifted to a sitting position, waiting, plucking grass and snapping twigs, something to chew or toss absently away. After a few minutes, I tried to stand, but my legs shook, forcing me back to the ground. Growling, I rolled onto my knees and attacked my pack, pulling out a prednisone bottle. I rolled the bottle in my palms, mentally reciting a litany of side effects.

Fuck it. I choked down six pink tablets, bitter but hope-tinged. No immediate benefit, I knew, but energy for later, climbing the rock or climbing down, maybe just the little umph I'd need to help me get home.

On my next attempt, I managed to stand and walk without too many stumbles or curses, but three hours passed before I reached the base of the Peak, and by then the sun was blazing. In front of a rock wall I tottered across a flat stone surface, realizing too late how unsteady I was. I fell hard on the rock and lay still for a while.

"Goddammit." I took a look at my skinned palms, but the sun was blasting me, so I rolled over and closed my eyes. I knew I needed to rest and cool down, but with heat building on the back of my neck I sat up. I couldn't give up now. The Peak was close, so close it unnerved me. I imagined the moves to come, some energetic, some delicate and balanced, and I knew I wasn't ready.

Although I still felt too hot, I got to my feet and started down a steep section before I could climb. My first few steps were better, but on my fifth step my right boot caught the rock, and I hopped and twisted before falling on my butt.

Fuck you. I started to scoot down the rock on my bottom, feet in front, hands behind, but on my third crab-like shuffle my body rolled to the left. Head downhill, I strained with my right hand holding my weight. I wanted to drag my feet under my body, but my legs felt like lifeless slabs of wood and didn't respond.

With my right arm weakening, I clawed my left hand into a crack in hopes I could lift my body. The maneuver worked. I swung my legs down to footholds and a minute later I sat upright, safe. After wiping the sweat from my face, I stood, wobbled, and had to grab a nearby boulder.

My usual route was right there, but the sun repelled me, glaring off the granite in waves. I teetered, panting and squinting, and abandoned my swearing and two-fisted bravado in the awful knowledge that I was about to fall.

I sat down to stare at my boots. Dying didn't seem like an option, but then neither did retreat. I gave myself time to cool off and waited for another alternative, but twenty minutes later with no shade, I was still as hot as sunburn. I reviewed my supplies – not enough water for another night, especially in this heat.

Dammit. No way, no fucking way.

Even though I managed to stand up, clenching my teeth, I still tottered. I stepped, but my right boot barely cleared the ground. I tried to steady myself by leaning against the rock wall, but my strength was ebbing, seemingly blowing out my mouth in short, hot breaths. My jaw remained tight, but sweat stung my eyes and dripped from my face. Then my legs crumpled, folding slowly until with a groan I had to sink onto the rock.

"Oh, shit." I coughed, choked and tried to spit, but I could only lean forward and drool. When I was finally able to sit upright and control my saliva, I began surveying the damage to my scratched hands. Torn nails and skin, swollen fingers that would open and close only with difficulty.

And then the world quieted. I shook my head and swallowed, considering. I could crawl. Yeah and fall, you fucker. It's true. Yeah, I know. I could wait for it to cool, then climb. Not realistic – it's already gonna be hard to make it in before dark. Fuck. I made it all this way, all this way for nothing?

I looked across the canyon to Moses Mountain and to the road that twisted up the mountain's lower reaches. I closed my right eye, blocking the road from my vision, and saw the wilds as they must have been centuries before. From somewhere overhead, a hawk issued a piercing cry.

I'd made it all this way, made it to the top many times. Why couldn't I do it again? Yeah, I could do it again, on another day. Yeah, a cooler day, a day earlier or later in the year, April, May, or, maybe, October. The creek would be higher in April, the rocks slicker, but the Peak would be cool, cold even, and my legs would work. They'd work well in the cold.

"I'll be back."

But before I turned, before I started the long and sensible trek home, I studied the Peak, memorizing the path, the cracks, and smiling at the sunlight that left an orange after-image before my eyes. Someday, I won't be reasonable or weak. Someday, my legs will work, my fingers and feet will find the cracks, and I'll climb swiftly – driven and reckless, moving ever upward, graceful, pausing only to grin or to pant at a small patch of sun. Someday, the light will brighten the rock, exposing the crevices and knobs, and on that day, that magical day in the spring or late fall, the rock will hold the night, and its coolness will run too deep for sweat or even hot spit. Someday.

Ursula

I prepare the red curry, as opposed to the yellow curry. Restaurants in this country tend toward the yellow curry, but to me that is not a legitimate curry. I use a tomato base, braised onions, masala, cilantro, serrano peppers, garlic, chili powder, a little tamarind, and a small quantity of turmeric. Crab curry, properly prepared, is especially divine, but Clint complains that he will starve to death while eating it. He lacks the patience for breaking the pieces, delicately cracking open the shells, and removing the tender morsels. With Clint it's always rush, rush, rush, not proper eating, no enjoyment.

So I make chicken curry for Clint, yet many times he is simply not interested. Once near the end of his residency, I prepared some scrumptious chicken curry to celebrate his return from Dennison, but he didn't enjoy the meal at all. He picked at the edges, dabbling, as if dissecting a frog in anatomy class. I finally took away his plate.

I knew that he had not reached the top of Dennison Peak, but I could not fathom his distress. He climbed almost the entire way, extraordinary for a chap who normally walked with a cane. He still needed food, and he should not have allowed such an inconsequential event to spoil his appetite.

CHAPTER TWELVE

Living in the Real World

Ursula

When we first arrived for Clint's job interview with the Indian Health Service or IHS, he stepped from the rental car and looked out over the flat, windswept land essentially devoid of vegetation except for prairie grass and sagebrush. He coughed in the frigid air, kicked at the frozen earth, and grumbled, "There's no way in hell I'm coming here."

But that was before we traveled further to tour the fine new IHS hospital. The hospital and the clinic were bustling, patients seemed extremely gracious, and everyone was smiling and sociable. In short order, Clint changed his mind, and after a number of discussions, I acquiesced to a two-year stint living in the Great Plains.

Admittedly there were benefits: loan repayment, a hefty salary, an enormous home, fairly negligible living expenses, and health insurance. Even so, though, when I was home alone – as was often the case – I gazed out the window at the snowdrifts and forlorn expanse and felt an almost overwhelming urge to weep. At such times, I had to remind myself that we could drive to Billings in less than two hours – assuming the highway remained open.

As for fine cuisine, our small town had little to offer. What restaurants there were all served fast food, about as noteworthy as gruel. On the reservation where Clint worked, the two eating establishments featured Indian tacos, and while even those surpassed the fare available in town, I found them disappointingly bland.

So after we moved to the plains most of our dining was

done at home. Now and then we traveled to the state capitol or another larger town where we could have Chinese food or dine at Red Lobster or Olive Garden. The food there was decent, but nowhere was there an Indian restaurant – no curry, rice, and dhal, no roti and tandori, no samosas and pappadums.

And it was not merely the surroundings that unsettled me. Clint was working more than he should have. He was pushing on his personal accelerator for no apparent reason, as if he simply had to feel the wind on his face or had resolved to continue to the point of collapse.

College was finished. Medical school and residency were finished. He needed to take a bloody deep breath and relax, but he simply would not. More than once, I attempted to discuss the matter with him, but he was dismissive or worse.

Ursula

"Ursh! I'm sick! Hurry!" I yelled and heard Ursh's footsteps on our hardwood floor – thumping, thumping too heavy for such a small creature – but it was too late. I vomited just as she opened our bedroom door, and it splattered and spread on the floor, bilious and foul.

"Don't move," she said. "I can handle it. Merely stay where you are." Ursh mopped and cleaned, her face pinched tightly even as she raced, bucket in hand, to the bathroom. I heard water splashing in the sink.

"I'm sorry, Ursh."

"It's quite all right. You can't help being sick. We now have a pan for the next time."

"Hopefully, there won't be a next time. I just need a second to regain my strength." The water had stopped running, and Ursh was back with a wet washcloth. It was cold on my lips and face, and so was Ursh's hand on my forehead. I closed my eyes. The darkness was as quiet as a library but felt a little spooky, as if peopled with dark spaces and shapes that both sheltered and threatened.

"You are burning with fever. I'll bring some Motrin and

some ice."

"I'll take Motrin, but I'm chilled. No ice, no ice." I grimaced but kept my eyes closed – no lights, no buzzers, no bouncing balls.

"Very well, but you know how you are when you run fever. You might need to go to hospital." She stood in front of me, pondering. Without looking I knew she was frowning.

"I'm not going in. Nobody needs to know anything."

"What's anything? Everybody already knows that you're ill."

"Yeah, but they don't need to know all my business."

"What might that be? That you have MS? I think that your secret's rather obvious, thanks to your cane."

"No, nobody needs to know that I'm on prednisone, that I can't move when I run a fever, or anything else for that matter."

"Well, as you wish." I heard her footsteps go to the kitchen, then a moment later she was back with Motrin and water. I swallowed and spoke, keeping my eyes shut. "Okay, just let me take a nap." Soon I was drifting, rocking and swaying in clingy covers and sticky sweat.

A bell was ringing, ringing, ringing. The hall was empty at my old elementary school, and a door was closing. I rushed and made it inside the doorway to the back of the class. Ms. Nelson was talking, pointing toward the chalkboard, asking questions. I moved toward my desk, slowly, quietly, hoping nobody would turn around. Ms. Nelson looked at me but didn't seem to see, and I was almost at my desk when a girl stopped me – a cute girl, strangely familiar, with dark, haunting eyes and playful fingers that touched my hand. She stood in front of me, asking questions and smiling, reassuring me with her eyes, her touch.

I glanced toward my empty desk, and when I looked back, the girl had become Lisa, my girlfriend of long ago. She wanted to know why I wasn't wearing clothes. I looked and saw it was true, but the whole class was now looking, even Ms. Nelson, and as the laughter started, I opened my eyes.

"Ursh, I'm sick again." I leaned over the bed as bile splattered into the pan, then I felt my bowels empty onto the sheets.

"Oh, shit, shit-shit-shit."

"There is no need for panic. Everything is quite all right."

"No, it's not. I just pooped in the bed – diarrhea and it's all over. Shit!" Before I could say more, I puked again and again until there were only dry heaves.

"Do not attempt to move. I shall devise a way to clean you."

I tried to get my head back onto the bed but couldn't move. My eyes closed, and even though I heard Ursh running water and opening cupboards in the bathroom, I was already far away at my first big track meet. The loudspeaker blared: "FINAL CALL FOR THE MEN'S SPRINT MEDLEY RELAY." I was tense and could taste the adrenaline as surely as I could smell the rubbery tarmac and the freshly mowed grass. People were screaming. The race was close.

The baton passed once and then again, and I stepped onto the track, hopping and prancing, anticipating the final 800 meters. The baton came closer and closer. I could barely breathe.

"Your skin is burning. I hope that Motrin is effective. After I clean you, as best I can, I'll work toward removing the sheets."

"Uh, sure, yeah, uh, oh." I had the baton now, and my legs were pumping. I was leading, and my mind was blank, engrossed by my breathing and the race of rubber under my feet. Only one thought, one goal, screamed in my mind, incessant and rapid. "Faster, faster."

"Pardon, I'm working as fast as I am able."

I finished the first lap, and the crowd was out of control, yelling so loudly that I barely heard my split – 57 57? 57? The number couldn't penetrate the riot of my mind, and dissipated in my labored breath.

My legs started to slow but just a little. The backstretch was quiet, as if separate from the meet, as if the race were already over. I felt disconnected but tried to refocus and gather myself for the sprint home. Two hundred meters to go – time to go, time to kick. My legs were heavy, tight, and I started to plod.

Falling

Adrenaline surged, accompanied by panic. Come on, come on. This is it!

"In a moment I'll pull you from the bed and remove the linen."

I rounded the curve, entering the final stretch, and the crowd noise exploded in my ears. My jaw was set and my eyes drawn, but the once-fluid motion of my stride was tightening into a stagger. My body began to sway, slowing even more.

I leaned forward, trying desperately to generate momentum, but my legs barely kept me upright. Fifty meters from the finish my head was swimming back and forth, and the crowd was a fire alarm between my ears. Still I fought, lurching for the tape, and it was coming, edging closer with each stumble. Then I dove for it, but the fall was too slow, as if gravity was tired too, and in an instant, a shape flashed by me.

My arms hung limp at my sides as my body crashed to the track, bouncing once before being still.

"Pardon the bump, but it is the only way I can move you."

All was pain, as I was lifted and carried away. The voices were many but distant and indistinct – meaningless chatter, like a lighted auditorium before the banquet. Or was it an opera? That was it – the moments before some magnificent spectacle, an event complete with costumes and orchestra, spotlights and sopranos. Soon face-painted divas would flutter and croon, but it hadn't started yet, and the people could barely wait, glancing toward the stage only to turn back regretfully. Some were stoic, while others spoke faster and faster, trying to critique a performance before it began.

Then dark hushed the room, and the people watched the stage – their eyes unmoving, unblinking lest they miss something dramatic or soulful or sad. Yet moment after moment the curtains remained closed. A rumble started, an uneasiness that swept through the theater like the roll of a bass drum. It hovered and spread in the dark, airy expanse before settling onto the rows of blue-velvet seats. When it started again a few moments later, it was louder, stronger, and accompanied by a splattering sound. Then I realized that the performance was over. I was under the bleachers vomiting.

I felt dizzy. The fans were yelling and stomping above my head. Something had gone wrong, terribly wrong. My body hurt. I didn't even want to think about how bad I looked. "FIRST CALL FOR THE WOMEN'S DISCUS." My head throbbed. A teammate was talking to me. I had been the anchor leg on the sprint medley relay. I had gone out too fast. I had collapsed at the end. I would get a medal for second, second, second.

The pounding and yelling started again with the next race. My teammate had to go, something about his bag. "FINAL CALL FOR THE MEN'S LONG JUMP." It was cool and shady under the bleachers, but I felt strange, sick, and much older than fifteen.

"I know that the floor's hard, but simply be patient."

"I'm okay. I'm not hurting as bad now."

"Hurting? Where might you be hurting?"

"Everywhere." The next moments were so quiet that I almost slept, almost forgot the second-too-slow fall.

"Might I summon an ambulance?" I knew Ursh was frowning, but I didn't open my eyes.

"No, no, I just need to sleep."

"In a bit, might you have the strength to reposition onto the bed?"

"Absolutely, positively, no way. I'll sleep right here."

"Well, I might be able to position a pad under your body."

"Um, yeah . . . yeah." I was already sliding, turning and falling, but slowly, like a body in a pool, rolling and drifting downward – an odd sensation, weightless, wispy, and peaceful. Then hot air ballooned to the surface in a wavy ring, but I was already sinking, like an empty tin can, into the depths of black.

When a voice came it wasn't really words, just sounds, raspy and senseless, emanating from some willful teen. Maybe he had just broken up with his girlfriend or lost his after-school job. He stumbled down an alleyway, mumbling and kicking his frayed Nikes in the dust – their fluorescent green brightness dulled. His speech was incoherent but painful and passionate, and although he shuffled out of sight behind a rusty dumpster, his voice grew louder, closer.

In a few moments glass broke, maybe the crack of a bottle on the curb, or the sound of a rock through a window. Whatever the source, silence followed, and when the voice returned, it was hoarse and tortured, coming from inside my own throat.

"Are you doing any better? Might you prefer something to eat?"

"I don't know, I don't know. Shit, I hate being sick. I just need to sleep."

"You've been sleeping a considerable time. Hold it! Do not move. You've toppled and broken your water glass. Please, do not move."

"I need some water. I'm so dry. Fuck that! I just need to get the fuck up." I started to move, contracting and contorting.

"Hold on, I need to remove the glass."

"I'm not waiting for shit. I'm getting up now." I slammed my palm onto the hardwood floor and tried to rise, but I was tangled in my blankets and slipping on the floor.

"Wait and let me help you."

"Fuck you. I'm getting up. I don't need help." I lifted my upper body but couldn't bring my legs under me.

"Let me push your legs."

"Then push my legs, dammit! I got nothing to push against, and I'm struggling here, and you're standing there looking dumb!" My arms collapsed, but I managed to twist onto my back as I fell.

"What now?"

"I don't know what now! My fucking legs won't work and my arms aren't much better." I grimaced and then let out a big breath, feeling the dryness of my throat. "Just let me rest a second."

"What if I called someone?"

"Like who? Santa Claus? I'm not going in, 'cause nobody needs to know my business. Fuck it. I'm getting up."

I rocked and strained, trying to roll. My face was on fire. Slowly, I rolled and ended up kissing the floor. I took a few deep breaths, then lifted my body, squirming to pull my legs under me. I felt Ursh pushing against the bottoms of my feet, trying to help. At last I made it to my hands and knees.

"You did it."

"Oh, shit, I'm gonna puke." I vomited but nothing came out. "Fuck you. I am not gonna be sick anymore." With a sudden surge of strength, I climbed onto the bed and collapsed, panting. Several moments passed in silence.

"Might you care to eat or drink something?" Ursh's words were soft.

"Yeah, some Gatorade and, maybe, some soup and more Motrin." I closed my eyes and felt my stomach settling.

"Let me first bring the Gatorade and Motrin, and then I'll prepare some soup." I heard her start to walk toward the kitchen.

"Ursh." I heard her stop. "Thanks. I'm sorry I'm an ass."

When she brought the Gatorade I drank two gulps and swallowed the pills before my stomach cramped, forcing me to stop.

"You need more fluid."

"I can't right now, maybe later. I just need to sleep some more." I was floating again, already rocking to and fro, and then shifting sideways and sinking. The deep was dark and now hot, and it swarmed over and enveloped me, clinging like a leech, until sleep became a listless struggle and dreams shriveled like green peaches in a drought.

When I awoke there were no voices, no fury, no thrashing or yelling nor pieces of clear glass. Instead, my breath came shallowly, straining through my hot-sand throat. I listened to it without feeling, like a bored spectator at a tennis match.

"Clint, are you finally awake?"

"Um, well, yeah, maybe."

"Might you like something to eat or drink?"

"Maybe."

I felt the glass against my lips and sipped some tepid Gatorade.

"Let me help you to sit up."

"I need to make it to the bathroom."

I rolled to the edge of the bed, where my arm dangled.

Falling

"Please be careful. You are about to fall from the bed."

"I know. That's how I'm gonna get on the floor and crawl to the bathroom."

"Might I bring a pad?"

"I don't need a pad. Watch and learn, you silly Creature."

I smirked with momentary bravado but then felt the weakness return. I took a breath, squirmed, shifted, and dropped to my elbows and knees.

"Are you hurt?"

Without a word, I started to crawl toward the toilet, and after two brief rests, one on hardwood and one on tile, I made it and eyed the porcelain warily.

"How might I help?"

I strained to rise but fell back. "I need you to help me get my legs under me and then to help me get my fucking butt on the pot."

In the ensuing struggle, as Ursh groaned and pulled, I managed to reach the seat.

"Good job. Thanks, Ursh."

"You simply have to eat. I'll warm the soup." She left, as if she expected another sudden thud, and then I was alone. Outside the window, the barren landscape marked the end of the town's gravel roads and wind-bent fences. The sky was overcast, and the shadows stretched long, but I could see a long way across the fields. My focus shifted.

The urge to void was present, persistent, not agony but not easily ignored. I pushed on my lower belly and imagined a familiar waterfall, but nothing came, and I stared out the window again.

The prairie grasses were short, dry, and bunched, durable, brown and close to the ground. Yet in places scraggly flowers clung to islands of dark soil, their pale petals fluttering in the relentless wind. There were no trees, no cover, and still no tinkles in the bowl.

"Damn." A long, striped drinking straw sat on a nearby shelf, a remnant of a fast-food meal. I considered catheterizing myself. It was within reach but too flimsy and, of course, not sterile. No, bad idea.

"Clint, I have some soup — what's the matter?"

"I feel like I need to take a leak, but I can't go."

"Why don't you simply give it some time and try to eat some soup?" She made as if to spoon out the soup for me.

"I don't need you to feed me."

I was more tired than irritated as I took the bowl of broth, but after the third spoonful my stomach rebelled. "Here, hurry." I pushed the soup toward Ursh before soup and drool hit the floor between my feet.

"Shouldn't I call an ambulance?"

"I don't need an ambulance. I just need—" I was distracted, looking outside at a small whirlwind that kicked up dust. "Shit, a little bit more time." I breathed deeply in and out. "Let me go back to bed and sleep this off."

"Are you absolutely certain that you do not need an ambulance?"

"Yeah." I was crawling again, yet I couldn't recall getting off the toilet. Oh shit, the bed's so high. "Ursh."

"I'll help. Try to climb."

"Don't hurt yourself, Creature."

"One, two, three, go, go, go."

We got me up and I flopped onto the bed. "See, I don't need an ambulance. Just let me sleep awhile and I'll be fine. I'm invincible."

I smiled, drifting but not sinking, into more hallucinations. More light than dark, then the orchestra sounded, and an exciting array of dancers and singers stepped forward, their rainbow costumes shining and flowing as they pranced about the stage. More rushed in, racing faster and faster, until the vibrant mass started to undulate as dancers dove in and out, some running, some flying, until there were no more dancers or singers. Pure color and sound merged into a lusty and pulsating vortex, and gradually this vortex engulfed all sound, all color, until only the motion remained.

But the center wouldn't hold, and bright strips started to fall away, softening and dripping like sorbet in sunshine. And then the movement faltered, spinning slower and slower until it died amidst the litter on the dimly lit stage. I stood, cheering, applauding, until I saw that the auditorium was deserted – rows and rows of empty seats in stillness, in darkness, the only sound of someone crying, childlike and lonely, a long way away.

"Clint, please awaken. I think you need to awaken. I'm becoming quite concerned."

"Oh, well, um —" I tried to move. "Jesus." I kept my eyes closed.

"What's the matter?"

"I feel terrible." I opened my eyes briefly. "What day is it?"

"Wednesday night."

"No, what, don't mess with me."

"I swear; today is definitely Wednesday."

"What happened to Tuesday?" This time my eyes stayed open.

"Well, on Monday, Tuesday, and Wednesday for that matter, you were ill, vomiting, thrashing about, and sleeping."

I grimaced and groaned, closed my eyes for a bit. I wanted to talk, but words wouldn't come, only sighs.

"Do you finally wish for me to call an ambulance?"

"Go ahead. Yes, call 'em now. And Ursh — we need to tell them I'm on prednisone."

"But I thought you preferred —"

"I know, I know, but I'm gonna need stress doses of steroids at this point." My eyes closed, as Ursh left to call.

Soon the wind was howling and swinging the door, banging it against the wall. What the hell? A storm must be coming. Ursh, Ursh, can you close the door? Ursh — oh, I didn't see you. She was frowning, looking a little angry, and she grabbed the door and slammed it shut. Hey! You don't have to slam the door; some of us are trying to sleep.

"Doctor Pearson, Doctor Pearson, which hospital do you want to go to? The one on the rez, or the one here in town?"

I was in an ambulance now, the air a furnace on my face. "Oh, shit, oh, oh — what?"

"Which hospital shall we go to?"

"The closest hospital, the closest."

I tried to stay awake by focusing on my breathing, but the air was hot in my throat. I can't breathe it. I can't, I won't. I refuse. Fuck you. Get me some cold air and don't forget the IV. I need fluids too, a 500-cc fluid bolus. Don't forget my vitals. But I need cold air now, now before the other shit. That's better, much better.

"We'll take him to the hospital down the street, Mrs. Pearson."

For Christ's sake, Ursh, stop slamming doors. She thinks just because she's married to a doctor she can go around slamming doors. If you slam the French doors, you might break the glass. That'll cost us a pretty penny. Sure, go run off in the car just because I bitched about slamming the doors — All right, all right, it's okay, Ursh. Just slow down.

"Bighorn, we're en route with a thirty-three-year-old male with diarrhea and vomiting for three days. He's dehydrated and delirious."

Great, now I'm delirious just because I don't like doors being slammed. Why don't you talk to Ursh? She knows she slammed it. She's probably sorry. But she's too embarrassed, and that's why she drove off.

"Temperature one oh four point four, heart rate one forty eight, and pressure seventy over palp. We're running normal saline wide open."

Liar, you didn't bother to take my vitals, and there's no I.V. running. I don't know about these new paramedics. You can't trust 'em. But, crap, it's getting hot again. They need to open a window. Got to blow it away, blow the heat away. Breathe in cool, breathe out hot. Huff and puff like the big, bad wolf. No, it's too much heat, too much exhaust in the garage. Let it out quick. It's making me sleepy — Sleep it off — No — Yes — No — Yes — Whatever — just sleep —

"I'm Doctor Ostasky. Can you wake up for me?"

"What?"

"I'm Doctor Ostasky. Can you tell me what happened?"

"Whaddya mean?" My eyes wouldn't open.

"Try to wake up and talk to me."

"I've been puking, having fevers, diarrhea. What else is

there to say?" Something else sat in my mouth, something stuck between my teeth.

"I understand you have multiple sclerosis, and you haven't urinated in several days?"

My eyes opened. "Yeah, I can't pee, and I'm normally on prednisone, twenty milligrams a day. I'll need stress doses of steroids."

The effort of speaking left me drained, and I was glad when a nurse stopped me to check my temperature. But my panting mouth had trouble holding the thermometer. I closed my eyes, feeling the hot exhaust blowing once again against my face. Breathe it away, breathe it away, huff and puff, huff and puff. I'm blowing; I'm moving air.

"One oh six point two."

But the air's too hot. I can't keep breathing it. I need help. Ursh, come back, come back. I don't care if you slam doors. I break glass too. Pieces are jagged and hard to see sometimes. Like flashes, like flashes too fast or too blurry. Just don't hurt yourself, don't frown. The car's revving, and the garage is closed. Slip away, slide away slowly. I know I can't breathe anymore, but I'm trying, trying hard.

Sometimes the wind's gotta blow even if flowers don't. Even if petals fall. But the show's gotta start, just got to. If only there's room. Where do I sit? What's the number on my seat? It's too dark to see much, but I feel the velvet, the smoothness on my fingers. Where are the lights? Where are the dancers? Just wait, even if you don't have time. Something must happen, must. Sometimes a cry is all you get, but not all there is. There's always more, more space, more glitter.

I'm floating now, floating away and drifting, sad but only a little, like a touch remembered but not felt. And that sound? Do you hear it? Like wind, soft and oh so eerie, like wind, wailing and distant. Listen. Sounds almost like a wolf, injured and howling in pain, a little scary, perhaps, but nothing but wind, only wind.

Ursula

Clint's serious illness shook him up a bit. Afterwards, he was quieter, not feeling so invincible, and he started to speak earnestly of the need to wean from the prednisone. But his illness disturbed me as well, more than I cared to admit.

I remember his face, utterly pale and drawn, quite frightening to me. He was dehydrated, and they gave him liter upon liter of fluid and put a tube into his bladder so that he might urinate. Incredibly, they inserted a tube through his penis into his bladder, and Clint slept through the entire procedure.

I waited and waited for Clint to stir. I half-expected him to make a joke, to say something silly: "You'll need the extra-extra long tube for this job." But he never opened his eyes – not a sigh, not a grimace, certainly not a smile.

More than a day later, when he finally did begin to rouse, it seemed a dreadfully long time before he became coherent. He mumbled and tossed and pulled at his gown, and I was afraid his condition might deteriorate at any moment. I whispered to him and touched his face, but it was quite some time before he awakened. And that was not characteristic of Clint.

At first he asked the usual questions: "How long have I been here?" "What'd the doctor say?" "How high was my fever?" Utterly exhausted, talking depleted him further. Once he sighed and tried to reach toward me, but his hand just flopped on the bed. So then I lifted his hand, pressed it to my cheek, closed my eyes, and began to gently rock to and fro.

A short time later when I opened my eyes, his face was stricken and strangely sad.

"Would you mind if I walked you to the door and kissed you goodnight?"

It was the question he had posed at the end of our first date.

Then he laughed, a heart-rending half-laugh laced with longing and sorrow, and in short order tears began to fall. I leaned over the bed and soon we were both weeping, holding each other, touching, remembering days long before hospitals or even bona fide beds.

CHAPTER THIRTEEN

Fathers

And I know a father
Who had a son.
He longed to tell him all the reasons
For the things he'd done.
He came a long way
Just to explain.
He kissed his boy as he lay sleeping.
Then he turned around and headed home again.
-- from Paul Simon's "Slip Slidin' Away"

Clint

A hint of fear hovered in the father's voice.
"Is he doing all right? There's no problem, is there?"
His name was Paul Bear Skins, he was Cheyenne, and he would eventually entertain me with stories of drinking and fighting and growing up on the reservation.

But this was no time for stories. This was his first baby, and he stood at his wife's side holding her hand and watching as the nurses rushed to rub and dry his newborn son.

The baby had been delivered with no perineal tears. The newborn was in good hands, and everyone should have been able to relax, but Paul was obviously worried.

I got to my feet as well, not smoothly and swiftly, but I made it by grabbing a stirrup. I could see one nurse, Cathy, feeling the baby's umbilical cord, another, Gina, flicking the baby's foot.

"I don't know 'bout this." Paul was worried. "Dr. Pearson, don't you need to do somethin'?"

"Cathy, what's the heart rate?"

Without turning from the baby, she replied, "One ten. He just needs to wake up. Do you want to give the Narcan?"

"Yes, go ahead and give point four milligrams." I knew that the nurses didn't really need me, but I wanted to reassure Paul. I grabbed my cane, shuffled to the warmer, and reached the baby's side just as Gina finished injecting the Narcan. The room was quiet.

Paul spoke again. "Dr. Pearson, why ain't he cryin'?"

I reached for the Ambu bag. "He will, don't worry." I positioned the mask and squeezed the bag, forcing air into the baby's lungs. His little chest rose and fell in time with a whoosh of air.

Paul watched intensely as we worked. "Breathe, Daniel, come on, breathe. Come on, son, breathe."

Cathy read my eyes. "Heart rate one thirty."

Now Karen, the mother, reacted. "Oh, God, breathe, Daniel, breathe. What's happening? I can't see. Is he okay?" I heard her trying to rise on the bed, and I knew she still had the umbilical cord dangling between her legs.

"He's all right. He just needs a little help."

Everything was fine, wasn't it? We were just bagging the kid. The mother had been given pain medicine before pushing the baby into my arms, sooner than expected. In a minute or less the Narcan would do its job, and then it would be "Ooh!" and "Aah!" and "Look at his tiny toes!" But fear had overwhelmed the new parents, and no amount of reassurance could unclench their hands or stop their pleading.

Paul urged him on. "You can do it, Daniel. Breathe, son, breathe. You can do it. You're Cheyenne. You've got to breathe."

"Heart rate one thirty." Cathy's tone was matter-of-fact.

"It's all right. Paul, Karen, he's doing fine. It'll just take a little while.""Please, Daniel, you've got to breathe! Breathe, damn it, breath, son, come on!"

I could hear Karen sobbing, as Paul exhorted the tiny boy.

"Color's good. Starting to get some grunting." Gina's calm voice did little to quiet the room.

Falling

"Come on, son, you can breathe! I know you can. Now's the time to breathe, Daniel. You can do it."

Behind me I heard Karen make a strange sound, half-choke and half-cry, and briefly wondered if we were bagging the wrong person. I half-turned, checking on her. "Karen, it's okay."

Gina was smiling. "He's starting to perk up."

Paul began to yell, "Daniel, you can do it! You're Cheyenne. Breathe, breathe, breathe!"

And then Daniel sucked air. The mask muffled it, but it was unquestionably the prelude to a good, healthy scream. Then, and as Daniel wailed, I became aware that Paul had slumped toward the bed, toward Karen.

At the time I didn't think much about it. I knew that parents sometimes get excited at a birth, but still I was surprised a short time later, when I saw Paul and could tell he'd been crying.

"They just plain and simply should have come here, not the hospital in town." Dr. Whiting was shaking his head and frowning under his mustache. The Indian Health Service provided free healthcare but didn't like to pay for any services outside the unit.

"But the patient lives twenty miles away from here, and she was in severe pain. Where would you go, Jerome, if you couldn't walk from the pain?"

"Here."

"Fine, but if it were me, I'd go to the nearest hospital, same as she did." I felt my face getting warm.

"And you'd pay the bill."

"Not if I couldn't afford it."

Dr. Lionel Turner interrupted. "Hold on guys, time out. I have a letter here that the patient wrote. Let me read it:"

On the evening of March 20, I was at home watching T.V. when I started having bad belly pain. I have never had pain so bad and I couldn't stand up. My husband had to carry me to the car and he took me to the hospital in town. I'm normally seen at the reservation hospital, but I was really hurting and the local hospital was only two blocks away. They did some blood tests and an ultrasound and told me I had gallstones. I got some painmedicines and went home. A week later I got the gallstones taken out at the IHS hospital. I am requesting that IHS pay for my bill at the local hospital. I wouldn't have gone there if I wasn't hurting so bad.

The room was quiet for several moments. Then with a stark, thin-lipped expression, Dr. Mike Ledger, the medical director, spoke as if the money had to come directly out of his personal account. "We have absolutely no money in the contract-care budget to pay for questionable cases."

I knew the answer to my next question, but I couldn't resist. "If we're out of money, how have we gone almost a million dollars over budget?"

"Any money that's over the budget is taken from next year's funds. There's no way to spend what we don't have."

"Sure there is. We already have. I say we pay for what we're supposed to pay for and let the Feds sort out the money end of it. We don't have to pay for liposuction and tummy tucks, but stuff that's reasonable should be approved. If we do that and they see that the budget isn't covering it, maybe, they'll increase our funding."

"Or maybe they'll put us in jail." Dr. Whiting shook his head. "In California, it may be fine to spend money you don't have, but that's not the case here. I don't feel like going to jail just because you want to approve everything under the sun." On his final word he poked the air with his Mont Blanc fountain pen, which then slipped out of his hand.

"Oh, give me a break! Show me one doctor who has ever gone to jail for getting a patient what they need, especially when the doctor receives no personal benefit. I bet lawyers would stand in line, drooling, to take such a case."

Dr. Whiting was busy reaching, retrieving his pen. "Dr. Pearson, I'm not going to argue with you."

Dr. Turner sighed. "Let's vote. We've had enough discussion, and we're already late for clinic."

And so the week's last crisis came to a close and I didn't

even get a chance to try out some new cuss words. Ledger, Whiting, and most of the others voted no, and the request was denied – same story, different day. I just didn't understand these so-called doctors.

In what seemed like no time at all, we were meeting again to discuss more such cases.

"The first two requests are no-brainers. #459933 is a thirty-two year-old alcoholic male found in Billings and taken by ambulance to a hospital there where he was found to have a subdural. And #889222 – a fifty-nine-year-old female who had an MI while shopping in Billings and was taken to a hospital there. No choice, we have to pay for these."

Dr. Mike Ledger cleared his throat and shuffled some papers before going on. "Now for the elective cases. I have a request for a Dexascan as a screening test for a sixty-six-year-old female, #237657." He spoke the words with all the enthusiasm of a referee giving pre-fight instructions, stopping short of "Go to your corners and come out fighting."

Again, Dr. Whiting fiddled with his pen. "Has she ever been on steroids?"

I spoke softly, hoping that would carry my point. "It's become standard of care to get a Dexascan on all women over sixty-five to screen for osteoporosis." My face already felt warm.

"Do we have any money in the contract-care budget?" Dr. Whiting apparently was trying the same strategy, posing his question as innocently as a child asking about chocolate-chip cookies.

Dr. Mike Ledger answered. "Unfortunately, there's no money left until next year." He shrugged, then went on, "So we'll defer the Dexascan request. Next I have #579881 – a request for a back MRI as a prerequisite to surgery. It's Dr. Franklin's patient."

Dr. Tom Franklin checked his watch. "This patient says he's got pain, wants surgery, but he gets plenty of pain medication. I told him we don't have the money, but he wanted me to request anyway. So, what do we say?"

I looked at the request form, recognizing the name. It

was time to wake up. "Does this patient have any leg weakness, Tom?"

"Some."

"How about incontinence?"

"Some."

"Yeah, I think I've seen this patient a few times in clinic. Does he have erectile dysfunction?"

"I don't know."

"I can't remember for sure either, but I think he does. I think I gave him a script for Viagra."

Dr. Whiting couldn't wait any longer. "What's your point?"

"The point is this guy's got a terrible back and needs surgery yesterday. I think it's time to stop endlessly deferring and fooling around." I wanted to say "fucking around."

"We have no money. We shouldn't have to go over that again." Whiting put his pen in his shirt pocket as if he'd heard an imaginary bell.

"Well, Jerome, just today we had money for a guy with a subdural hematoma and money for a woman with a heart attack."

"Those were not elective cases." Whiting looked toward Ledger as if for support..

"Severe lower back pain, leg weakness, can't keep from pissing his pants, and can't get an erection – doesn't sound like an elective case to me."

"Well, it is. He's not going to die, and we have no money."

"Sure we do. We just don't want to run up the debt and draw the attention of the head honchos at IHS."

Whiting romped over my objections. "This discussion is useless. Let's vote."

So we did. Even though my corner lost the bout, I had some support, more than usual, so I tried not to feel bitter. The physicians at the IHS hospital where I was working exercised their rights and voted to safeguard the sanctity of the contract-care budget. Or, in bureaucratese, the request for #579881 was deferred for an indefinite period of time pending a change in budgetary parameters and/or a re-examination of the case's merits.

Ursula

The summer sky in our part of the plains is mesmerizing. It has a compelling distance and depth, like the ceiling of the Sistine Chapel or a planetarium. Under it one feels open, exposed, a bit vulnerable, even a little embarrassed simply to be present in such a grand theater. Absorbed in looking at it, I didn't hear Clint until he spoke.

"Hello, Creature."

"Hey, you're home already." I smiled at him and went inside, closing the door behind me. "I was visiting Shawna earlier. For the life of me, I cannot keep up with her. She is one busy bee." I strolled over to Clint, kissed him, and fell into a nearby chair.

"I don't know, Ursh. If Shawna kicked your ass, how you gonna handle kids?"

"I can do it with this." I rolled up my shirtsleeve to show my biceps.

"Okay, Schwarzenegger, don't keep me in suspense. What did the doctor say?"

"Can't do it. I am simply too old." I shrugged in playful exasperation. "Dr. Clark says my progesterone level is in the loo or someplace thereabouts."

"So you have luteal phase defect?" Clint can be a bit insufferable when he knows something.

"I guess. Yes, that is what he said."

"So does he want to start you on a fertility medicine like

Clomid?"

"I imagine so, he gave me a prescription. Might it be effective?"

"Probably, if you can get in the mood."

I smiled and did my best to wriggle seductively. "I am more than ready."

Later that night, though, we felt less smug. "You're tired," I said. "You've been working nonstop."

"Hold on, Creature, just give me a second."

Seconds elapsed, then minutes.

"Okay, okay, I think I'm ready."

I turned to kiss Clint and then to touch, but he certainly wasn't ready. "We both are in great need of rest. Let's try to sleep."

"Hold on, just give me a second. I can do this."

"I know, but we are both exhausted. Why can't we simply sleep?"

Clint looked dejected. "But I thought we were going to go for it and —" His words faded, then he shuddered and shook his head. "I thought we were going to have kids."

"We are. We are going to try, anyway. But you need to realize that I am no spring chicken and neither are you."

"Just because I'm tired tonight —?"

"It's not only tonight. It's other nights too. It's becoming quite difficult and you know it."

He pulled the covers around his body and peered out the window, although it was too dark to see much. I moved toward him, feeling for his hand beneath the linen. "Might you speak with Dr. Williams?"

"It's just too damned hot tonight. That's most of it, and I'm tired. But I'm not making excuses. I know what you're saying. I know. Fuck it. I'll talk to Williams and get some Viagra." He looked down into my eyes before shaking his head. "Fucking MS."

"That's it precisely. The MS is interfering with our fucking." My choice of words surprised even me.

Clint stared at me, but I was already giggling. Then we both began to laugh, laughing at each other as well as at our

tangled bedding. Linen and blankets were a mess, twisted and
bunched, untucked and hanging. But disorder was the order
of this particular night. Our laughter led to tickling, then to
touching, and then to kisses both tender and deep. And the night
became alive and truly hot, so hot that the twisted and sweaty
cover was no longer needed.

Clint

"Doctor Pearson, I can't feed myself 'cause I'm shaking
so bad, and I can't wake up when I take more medicine, and I
can't dress myself, and they told me I could get surgery to fix
the shakes, but I'm old and on a fixed income, and Indian Health
won't help, and I can't—"

"Hold it, Mr. Sandy, let's take one thing at a time. What
did the neurosurgeon say? I haven't got his report yet."

"He said I should get the surgery to stop the bad shaking
in my right hand. He said the surgery's pretty safe and I can
do it at my age. He said I'd still have some shakes, 'cause the
Parkinson's doesn't go away, but that I'd be a lot better." He
relaxed a little, took a deep breath, and managed a half-smile.

Neatly dressed and polite, Pete Sandy was an atypical
patient for me. He could have passed for a retired accountant
from the city or a retired high-school administrator, someone
involved but reserved, definitely old-school but not greatly
bothered by the younger generation's antics. He'd been a
salesman, a fisherman, and a runabout in his younger days, then
worked as an office clerk until his retirement five years ago. Now
he was slowing down and wanted to enter his twilight years as
gracefully as possible.

After he told me what he wanted, his jaw suddenly
tightened, then more words tumbled out, making his head bob.
"I've got Medicare, but they only pay eighty percent and the
surgery's twenty thousand dollars. I ain't got that kind of money
'cause I'm on a fixed income, and I can't work with this shaking,
and the Indian service says they won't pay, and they said I could
sell my place and go into the nursing home, but I won't do it. No

sir, I won't do it."

"Hold on a second, Mr. Sandy. What about increasing your Sinemet?"

"I can't do it. I take only so many a day."

"I know, but what if I gave you a bigger prescription?"

"If that's the case, I might as well go to the nursing home."

"Why? It won't cost you any more."

"I won't be good for nothing, might as well go to the nursing home."

"Mr. Sandy, I don't think you're ready for the nursing home. Let's just go up on your medicine."

"I can't do that."

"Why not?"

"I'll sleep all the time."

"Oh, the medicine makes you too sleepy. I get it." I began to see which one of us was a little slow. "Have you tried drinking coffee to stay awake?"

"I drink coffee all day, anyway. Always have."

So much for the recent report that coffee reduced the incidence of Parkinson's disease.

"Well, how bad is your hand shaking?"

"It's real bad. I can't eat. I drop food all over, see?" He pointed to a stain on the front of his shirt. "That happened this morning, and sometimes I got to change or even take a shower after I eat. And soup, forget it. I might as well dump the bowl in my lap, since that's where it ends up."

His description might have seemed humorous, but he was definitely not laughing. "I can barely dress myself. My son has to help me, and as for writing letters, forget it. I can't even write my name any more."

He grabbed a pen out of his shirt pocket and started looking for a piece of paper, his hand shaking so vigorously I was afraid he would stab himself or stab me.

"Okay, okay, I see it's really bad. You don't need to show me."

He gave up the effort but continued to shake, and his head continued to bob. When he tried to put the pen back in his pocket he only succeeded in marking his shirt before he dropped the ballpoint to the floor.

"It's okay," I said. "Just leave it. We'll get it later."

"See? Now I have to wash this shirt."

"Mr. Sandy, do you want to have the surgery?"

"I'm on a fixed income and —"

"No, if you could afford it, do you want the surgery – yes or no?" I could hear rustling in the adjacent room and knew time was short.

"Yes. I have to do something to stop this shaking."

"Then get the surgery. Medicare will pay eighty percent, and we'll worry about the rest later."

"But I can't afford —"

"If it were me, I'd get the surgery. You need it. It's safe. Get it."

"But what about —"

"Look, I can't promise you that Indian Health Service will cover your part. They may not, but I promise you I'll do all I can to get it covered. And if you don't get the surgery, you're just not going to get any better, period." I got to my feet slowly and shrugged to emphasize the point.

"All right, all right, I hear what you're saying." He stood with considerable jerking . "I know I'll never be much of an office person any more or a letter writer for that matter, but for crying out loud, I would like to be able to write a letter once in a while and balance my checkbook." He glanced down wistfully at his pen.

"I hear you. That's why you should get the surgery."

I walked over to the fallen pen and reached a hand toward it, balancing on my cane. I came close, but just as my fingers neared the pen, I teetered backward and had to regain my balance. Once I was steadier I tried again.

In that instance my patient's judgment was better than mine, for he said, "Let's forget about the pen. You'll only fall and hurt yourself, and there aren't any other doctors this close to where I live."

"I have a request for a Dexascan for #237657, a sixty-seven-year-old female who stepped off her porch and fractured her right ankle. It required surgery, and given the severity of the injury from such a mild trauma, it's believed that she has osteoporosis, which needs to be verified with a Dexascan before she starts Fosamax."

Dr. Lionel Turner looked up from his paper to add, "I think this should be approved. It's not a screening test."

Whiting looked bored, Mike Ledger sat stone-faced, and most of the others nodded agreement, but before the case was approved, I had to add a fact. "This is the same woman who was turned down for a Dexascan six months ago, and as a result, we didn't have her on Fosamax."

Brief murmurs unsettled the room, then Mike Ledger said, "Even if we had made the diagnosis and had put the patient on Fosamax, six months is not long enough to reverse osteoporosis. In all likelihood, she still would have broken her ankle."

That wasn't the point, but I nodded my head to show team spirit then introduced my idea. "I've been thinking of a way to take care of our patients on the deferred list. How many do we have now, Mike, seventy? Eighty?"

"Give or take, something like that."

"Now probably the vast majority will qualify for Medicaid, correct?"

"I don't know about the vast majority, but most probably would."

"Well, let's get them on Medicaid. That's all we have to do. Don't we have someone who does that, who helps patients fill out the paperwork for Medicaid?"

"The short answer to that question is no. Medicaid has a guy in the Billings office who comes out here once a week. Any patients interested would have to find him and get an application."

"Why can't we get someone to help sign up patients here?"

Dr. Whiting spoke up. "First, it's probably illegal to have someone whose job it is to get patients on Medicaid."

"All the hospitals in the country, except for IHS

hospitals, have someone to do just that, to get patients signed up for something. Otherwise they wouldn't get any reimbursement for many of their patients."

Ledger took up the oppositional stance. "Who do you have in mind to do this job, Clint?"

"Can't the tribe hire someone?"

"They could if they decided it was important and if they had the money. But IHS provides the healthcare, and for free, I might add. Even if the tribe wanted to implement what you're suggesting, which I question, they don't have the resources."

"We have offices right here filled with plenty of staff. Why don't we recruit someone, give them some training, and let them do something important?"

"The jobs here are federally designated, paid for with federal money. To change any job description without federal approval is illegal. It's clearly misappropriation of federal funds and constitutes fraud."

"So what you're saying is that Washington, D.C. runs everything here?'

"The short answer is yes. "

"Then what if we all wrote letters to Congress saying we needed this position? It probably wouldn't do a damn bit of good but—"

"Everyone here is a federal employee, and as such, prohibited from any type of lobbying effort such as you're describing. The long and the short answer is it's illegal."

"Okay, then let's get some information on this Medicaid guy who comes and get the word out. We can put flyers at the appointment desk, talk about the benefits, and encourage people to apply."

"We could do that, but there is a downside."

"What? It's a federal crime to make flyers on federal paper?"

"Some of our patients who obtain Medicaid are likely to go to outside providers and outside pharmacies. Then we'd have a much more difficult time keeping track of their medicines. Imagine our patients getting Percocet from doctors in town or even a hundred miles away. We'd have to spend a substantial amount of our time calling pharmacies to find out what our patients are getting and where."

"That just comes with the territory. It's normal practice in the outside world."

"Not here. Do we really want to introduce that headache when we don't have to?"

Not ready to give up, I said, "Of course — " then looked around and stopped short. Hardly a one of the doctors in the room gave any indication of taking my side. Most just seemed annoyed by this gung-ho, unsatisfied cripple, an unbalanced colleague on some goddamned crusade to save the world and make all the more work for them.

A moderate among them, Dr. John Nowill spoke as if for the group. "Your idea is intriguing, something we should all consider at length. Perhaps we can think about it on our own, then discuss it at a later date."

"Sounds good. We're out of time. Let's all get to where we're supposed to be."

I sat in place as the room cleared, staring at nothing but thinking of the future.

My moderate ally also lingered and sat down beside me. "Your idea, well, it's certainly something to think about. I agree the deferred list is too long."

I nodded. He went on. "When I first came here – it must have been nineteen years ago – I was like you, spirited and idealistic."

I glanced his way and managed a small nod. "I wanted to help my patients, and half the time, it seemed like IHS was working against me. But eventually, despite the poverty and the sad stories, you come to realize that it's just a job, no more, no less."

He stood and gave me a careful pat on the shoulder. "Well, I better get to my office."

I turned to watch him go. Nothing more about my idea ever turned up.

Ursula

A bit after daybreak on a cold December morning, I watched an ambulance stop in front of our house. Straightaway I opened the door and stepped outside, shivering at the top of our stairs despite my mukluks and fleece robe. A coating of new snow graced our lawn, our stairs, and our street, giving the neighborhood a fresh, clean appearance.

Clint opened the ambulance door, cane in hand, and stepped out into the snow. He managed to shut the door behind him, but in doing so he wavered, dropped his cane, and steadied himself by clutching the white picket fence around our yard. He smiled, waving up at me, as if his near-mishap was just a joke.

"Hold it, hold it!" I called out. "Try not to move until I clear the steps. I would prefer that you not fall. I would simply have to call the ambulance back."

I hurried out to shovel the snow, glancing in Clint's direction now and then. "Not yet, don't move."

He retrieved his cane and stood leaning on the fence and smiling at me.

"It's finished. Hurry. It's cold, cold, cold."

He climbed the stairs wearing a silly grin. "Is cold-cold-cold colder than just cold?"

"Of course, it is. Now mind the step, and do brush your boots on the mat."

He came into the house and sat down at the kitchen table.

I sat down too, to await his explanation. "Okay, a journey to Billings and back does not take the entire night, so why might the ambulance be bringing you home?"

"Our car's out at the hospital. We'll get it sometime this weekend. But, oh, you're not going to believe it." He shook his head and began pulling off his jacket.

"Was there some mechanical trouble?"

"First, as you know, I had to ride with my patient on the ambulance to Billings." He had finally shed the jacket. "My patient who had a kidney infection had really low blood pressure, and I started her on a dopamine drip. Then she had a small heart attack and had to be transferred to Billings. Well, if a patient's on a dopamine, the doctor has to go along – some dumb ambulance rule. So here I am traveling down to Billings – "

"Was the patient all right?"

"Oh, she was fine, no chest pain. Blood pressure was low but stable, no problem. So anyway, here I am at two in the morning, just hanging out on my way to Billings, rolling along the highway, snow on the ground, dark as can be, and I'm just hanging out – "

"I do believe that I more than have the picture"

His eyes grew brighter, his face more animated. "Suddenly we came to a car in the middle of the freeway, across both westbound lanes, on fire. I'm not talking smoldering smoke and a little flame under the hood. This car is burning. Flames reaching ten, twenty feet in the air, with explosions shaking the car's fiery frame. The paramedic stopped the ambulance, then backed up."

"Oh, good Lord, do not tell me that people were trapped in the car?"

"No, no, the two occupants, a couple of young Indian guys, were outside, drunk off their asses, trying to throw snow on this inferno. My patient, she can't see and asks why we've stopped. I told her, 'It's nothing to worry about, just a, um, massive fire in the middle of the highway.'" Clint began to laugh.

I was definitely losing patience. "What bloody happened?"

"Well, about this time, one of the guys sees the ambulance and comes running over. The paramedic riding shotgun gets out to help, but the guy runs right by him and jumps in the front of the ambulance. I guess he got a little smoke inhalation to go with the booze or, maybe he was just freaking out. Anyway, he yells, 'Oh, Jesus, I'm dying!' and then he passed out, boom, just like that, out cold in the – "

Clint doubled over with laughter, unable to speak.

I stomped my foot and had thoughts of throttling my husband. "Was the man injured in some way, or not?"

Falling

Clint shook his head, still laughing too hard to form words.

"Then quite possibly we should concentrate on breakfast." I stood up.

"Okay, okay, let me finish. The guy could run over and jump in the ambulance so, obviously, he wasn't dying, but we checked him out just to make sure. Then his buddy came over, and we examined him as well. Then we were stuck, waiting for over two hours before firefighters could come and put out the car and move it."

"How did your patient fare?"

"Fine, seeing the cardiologist as we speak."

"And the two Indians?"

"Fine, just drunk. They claimed that some mysterious, strange but sober white guy picked them up. They said he was bald and old, had thick Coke-bottle glasses, and called himself Shy or Shi or something like that. They said that when the car quit and caught fire, this creepy driver jumped out, ran into the dark, and just disappeared." Clint cupped his hands and then opened them to find them empty. "Poof, vanished forever into the dark and unforgiving tundra of the Great Plains."

"Does this driver even exist?"

"Probably not, probably just a cover to avoid getting busted for drunk driving, but if the guy did exist, it's possible he walked to the eastbound side, caught a ride back, and is just now planning to terrorize our thriving metropolis."

I rolled my eyes. "What would you like for breakfast?"

"Anything. I'm so sleep-deprived and hungry that I'm rummy."

"Really? I hadn't noticed."

I walked to the stove, turning on a burner before finding a pan and opening our nice, new refrigerator for some butter and eggs. "Are you completely certain that you want to leave here?"

"Yes, I'm sure. I'll miss the patients, but, yeah, I'm sure. I already let Mike know we'd be leaving come August."

He got up and came toward me, but I turned toward the stove. "What did he say?" I grabbed a spoon and scooped butter into the warming pan.

"Not much, just thanks for letting him know so soon."

"Are you saying that he did not so much as ask why?" I jostled the pan as the butter melted and spread. It smelled enticing.

"Not really. It probably wasn't a surprise." Clint patted my bottom. "But, hey, remember that nonprofit group I told you about in California? They're looking for a doc, and several places in Oregon need docs too. The difficulty is going to be prying you away from the bright lights of this fine place."

"I believe I'm quite pryable." I looked down and behind me where he had touched me. "And even pliable, if you're extraordinarily nice."

"Hey, baby, I'm nice. I'm always nice to you."

I smiled and went on with my cooking. Into a bowl, I cracked an egg, then I added milk, green peppers, cilantro, and spice, and began to stir. I sensed Clint moving closer but continued to stir.

Lightly and lazily, he embraced me from behind. The pan was getting hot, and I spoke without interrupting my work. "After breakfast, we shall put your happy pills to the test."

Clint

Freddie Broken Bow looked nervous. Before morning report ever started he was fumbling in his lunch sack, pulling out a sandwich, then a soda before frowning and putting them back. Finally he pulled out a shiny red apple, inspected it, buffed it, smiled, and stuck it back in the bag too. Must not have been hungry.

The week before had brought an angry storm with pelting hail, chipping paint off the rusty cars on the rez, even cracking a couple of windshields. It lasted for five days, blowing paper trash and styrofoam cups across the schoolyard and tumbling the empty bottles behind the grocery store that had held 40-proof Listerine. On the third day one of the area's few tall trees, a cedar snag, surrendered its lifelong struggle against the wind and crashed to the ground near the old tribal voting site. Luckily everybody was over at the new site so nobody was hurt.

When the storm finally blew east it left a soggy mess of election flyers and stubby receipts, crumpled scraps testifying to a people's anger.

Now with sunshine filtering through the blinds at the hospital's conference room, the usual group of physicians took their seats, while Freddie Broken Bow remained standing and tried to explain.

"Before you guys get started on today's business, I've got an announcement to make. As you may or may not know, a new tribal council has taken office, and they have made a number of surprising and, um, ridiculous recommendations. None of these really affect you guys, but you should know."

"Oh, boy, I can't wait to hear what these Einsteins came up with." That was Dr. Whiting, cynical as usual.

"First, the tribal council has recommended the removal of the head administrator, Timothy Dunlap, as well as other IHS administrators, Jude Redman, Dave O'Malley, and Louise Menendez. In addition, the council has recommended the removal of medical director, Dr. Ledger, as well as Dr. Franklin."

"I knew I should have prescribed more Percocet." Laughter followed Dr. Franklin's remark, but some of the chuckles sounded uneasy.

A comprehensive discussion of the tribal council loomed, but Dr. Ledger kept the group on track. "Well, thanks for the information, Fred, but none of us is employed by the tribe, and we have a lot to cover this morning."

The first two cases were typical, a request for a total knee replacement and an appeal to have gallbladder surgery at another place – both denied. I was daydreaming, imagining my upcoming trip to Oregon and Northern California, and somewhere, in the back of my mind, calculating the number of these meetings I had left to endure.

A doctor's voice broke through my thoughts. "I have a request for #911321 for deep cortical stimulation. This patient has Parkinson's, and he's already had the surgery. Medicare and his supplemental insurance paid for most of it, but now he wants us to cover his co-pay. I saw this guy about a year ago and told him we didn't have the money, but apparently he went ahead and had the surgery, so now he wants us to pay."

I was fully awake. "Well, hold it. I think I can add a couple of details. This patient's on a low fixed income, and his right hand used to shake so that he couldn't feed himself. The neurosurgeon evaluated him and said he was a perfect candidate for deep cortical stimulation. Since the procedure he's much better, only a little shaky, and he can feed himself and write letters, the two things he most wanted to be able to do."

The administrator backed me up. "Yeah, I know this guy, and he's so much better. The improvement has been remarkable." He often attended these meetings but rarely made comments. Now he was smiling and nodding.

"That's all very well and good, but I told him he's got to pay his share."

"With what, Jerome, stones?" My face was already warm.

"If he didn't have the money, he shouldn't have gotten the surgery."

"Maybe you're right, Jerome, but I thought that's why we're here, to help people who can't even feed themselves."

"How much money are we talking about?" Dr. Turner, like many of the others, probably wanted something less abstract than "why we're here."

"To be exact, we're talking twenty percent of twenty thousand, four hundred and seventeen dollars. Give me a second." Mike Ledger was calculating on his new Palm Pilot – his stylus tapping on the small screen. "And then he's got supplemental coverage for eighty percent, so his total is exactly eight hundred sixteen dollars and sixty-eight cents."

Eight hundred dollars was enough for a mortgage payment on a nice three-bedroom house in town, enough for a down payment at the Ford dealership, enough to further erode an overdrawn contract-care budget. But the Palm Pilot didn't compute the fact that a new tribal council was making resolutions, and that eight hundred dollars was only a fraction of a physician's biweekly check, even at our hospital, even after taxes.

The mood shifted subtly.. Dr. Johnson, a woman who normally slouched through these meetings, was paying closer attention. Lionel Turner looked bright-eyed despite taking call and delivering two babies, and even though Jennifer Posh's vacation was only one week away, she closed her *Travel & Leisure* magazine.

Ledger responded. "The patient could have increased his medicine to control his shakes."

I felt the flush in my face as I answered. "He tried that, but the higher dose of Sinemet made him too sleepy."

"He could have waited until we had money."

"He's seventy years old, he can't wait for twenty years while we putz around and debate." I wanted to say "fuck around" and "masturbate," but I restrained myself.

Lionel Turner tried to obtain some closure. "I think we've all heard enough, so —"

"I told him what would happen, and I say —" Dr. Whiting tried to rekindle the discussion only to be blocked by John Nowill.

"Let's vote, Jerome."

The tally was close, but for once we renegades prevailed.

"Clint, are you seated?"

"Sure, I'm sitting. What's up, Creature?"

"I'm having twins."

That conversation happened early in Ursula's pregnancy, and for five months afterward she endured morning sickness at breakfast time, sciatic-nerve pain in a too-low bed, and finally a six-week stay at a Billing's hospital complete with hospital food, pills, and terbutaline injections.

By the time of delivery, seven and a half months along, she was still small but bigger for her, one hundred and thirty-five pounds and contracting more than ever.

Her obstetrician, Dr. Dave Jackson, sat at the foot of her bed ready to do his job. With his head up and hands hidden under the drape, he worked carefully by feel. "She's going – eight centimeters dilated. Let's get the epidural and get ready to deliver in the O.R."

"C-section?"

"No, vaginal, but in the O.R. so we can section if we need to. And I need the ultrasound in there, as always."

Everyone got busy. One nurse called the anesthesiologist, one called the pediatricians, one prepared the O.R. And all the while, Ursh was squeezing my hand and breathing as if something hot was burning her tongue.

Then we were in the O.R., where the stark lighting bleached every surface white. A doctor myself, I'd delivered enough babies to know all the things that could go wrong. It was a tense time.

"All right, you're complete. You can start pushing with the next contraction." Dave Jackson was smiling under his mask.

I smiled too. "You hear that?" I squeezed Ursh's hand, laughing. "Jasmine's almost here. You're doing it, Creature. You're doing great."

Ursula managed a smile of her own. "How much longer?"

"Not long, a few pushes and Jasmine will be here."

She eyed me suspiciously, but the next contraction started before she could say more.

"Not yet, Creature, let it build, let it build. Okay, deep breath and hold the push, hold it, longer, you're doing it."

Ursh exhaled and Dave took up the cheerleading. "Another deep breath, Ursula, and then push real hard."

When Ursh finished the contraction, I was surprised to see Jasmine's head. "Man, she's almost here. You're doing great!"

"Really? How much more?"

"Not much, another contraction or two."

"Here, Ursula, why don't you feel for yourself?" Dr. Jackson pointed toward Jasmine's head.

"Is that it?" Ursh's fingers caressed the dark, wet hair. "Oh my God."

In a moment she was pushing again but now grunting, strange and guttural.

"Here she comes, Ursula, almost there. Nice and steady.

Falling

Put your hands down here and catch her with me."

Ursh reached, but Dave Jackson did most of the catching. He clamped and cut the cord, then guided the baby to Ursula's hands.

Jasmine was small, pink, and alert. She looked about, blinking, not crying. Her new lungs must have liked the fresh air, for it flowed as easily as a ribbon in the wind. A pediatrician quickly swaddled the baby in a white towel and carried her to a warmer.

I sat stunned, staring and smiling. Dave Jackson delivered the placenta and was soon working on the second baby. It seemed there was trouble. "Quick, Belinda. What's on the monitor?"

"One ten."

"No, that's Ursula." Dave grabbed the ultrasound probe and placed it on Ursh's belly. Suddenly alarmed, I turned toward the screen. It was black and white but clear – four beats in six, four beats in six.

Six weeks is a long time to stay on guard. Dr. Jackson had done it, though, vigilant for six long weeks. Regular ultrasounds, pills, shots, and cervical checks followed by neonatal consults and more shots. But now none of it mattered. His response had to be decisive and perfect and swift.

"We've got to deliver this baby NOW! Push, Ursula. Push." Dave placed one hand at the top of her belly and one hand below to catch, then squeezed hard as if Ursh were a tube of toothpaste. Within seconds he was holding my gray and flaccid son, clamping and cutting the cord, and handing the baby to the white towels.

Then the pediatricians got to work and the only sound in the room was the repeated whooshes of air. Ursula and I could only watch and wait.

I remembered the sluggish motion, four beats in six, forty in a minute, but the pediatricians were only bagging, no chest compressions. I felt panicky, my mind spun with questions. Is his heartbeat better? Why doesn't he cry? What the hell's going on?

"How's he doing over there?" The only answer was

panting breaths too forced and loud to be real.

Ursh was staring with her mouth open and her fingers clutching the sides of her bed. She looked surprisingly fresh, ready to push, ready to endure, and ready to leave the hospital. She'd survived the winter's snow and now seemed ready to run in the sunshine, dance along the river's edge, laugh at the sunflowers. But summer was almost gone, and the work wasn't finished, not quite.

"Come on, Denali, I love you, breathe, breathe!" Ursh started but I was only a second behind.

"You can do it, Denali, breathe, come on, come on, breathe!"

The air continued to whoosh with no other sounds.

"Mommy's here, Denali. Breathe! Breathe for me."

"Come on, Denali, breathe, damn it, breathe! You can do it, Denali. Breathe."

The pediatricians worked intensely, confident, maintaining an intermittent sweep of air, but our voices were louder, stronger, and soon Denali heard his parents. He responded with a loud and wonderful wail.

The room came alive again with sound, and Ursh and I turned to each other. We were smiling and crying, smiling at our new babies and crying in gratitude.

CHAPTER FOURTEEN

Falling

All I know is that everything is not as it seemed.
But the more I grow, the less I know.
I have lived so many lives, though I'm not old,
And the more I see, the less I grow,
The fewer the seeds, the more I sow.
   -- from Nellie Furtado's "Try"

Clint

"Okay, Angel, take a deep breath and hold it. Bear down, push, push. Keep pushing."

With her face flushed, Angel fought to hold onto her air and effort, but soon the increased intensity of the contraction distorted her mouth and speech. "Oh, oh, shit."

The nurse wiped Angel's forehead with a wet cloth as the contraction eased, but Angel's face reddened. "Laverne, I'm sorry I lost control. I didn't mean to be disgusting."

"Oh, I've heard much worse. You keep concentrating on what you're doing, girl. You're doing great."

I offered my encouragement too. "You really are, Angel. The head's moving down. You'll deliver here in no time."

We were at my new hospital in California, near the Oregon border. One year previously, in August of 2001, I had taken a job there, and Angel was one of my first obstetric patients.

"Dr. Pearson, how's my baby doing?"

I looked to the monitor. "Absolutely wonderful, one happy baby."

The room was quiet, the only sound the monitor's soft

but rapid beeps.

Angel lifted her head to look at me. "Thank you for being here, Dr. Pearson, and for helping me. I really appreciate everything you've done."

"You're very welcome. I couldn't follow you for nine months only to miss—"

Angel's grimace halted my words. A contraction was building, and the end of her labor, like the baby's hair, was in sight. Ten minutes later the baby's head was doing its best to squeeze out of its confinement. Just one more nudge, one more tap, and it would slide clear and fall free.

"Push. You got it, just a bit more. You're almost there. Push a little more. You can do it."

Her next question brought me up short. "But the contraction's gone. Do I have to push, Dr. Pearson?"

"Well, uh, Laverne, are we picking up the baby?"

"One thirty, looks great."

I shook my head, smiling. "No, I guess, you don't need to push. Just relax. The baby's happy, and if you're happy, just kick back."

Angel sighed, closing her eyes, but I continued to stare, marveling at the little head bulging out of its prison.

Her rest didn't last long. "I have to push."

"Okay, give a little push, a little more. Okay, stop pushing while I suction. Okay, push again. You got it, beautiful. It's a girl." The baby was already crying as I fumbled to clamp and cut the cord. My hands shook more than usual, and the scissors seemed too small for my fingers. Soon Angel was holding her new daughter.

I exhaled, trying to stretch my fingers and crack my knuckles. To my relief, the next thirty minutes passed without tears, stitches, or bleeding, and no problems with the baby. Everything was as it should be.

"She's perfect, as beautiful as her mother, and she's all yours." I shucked off my latex gloves. "What's her name?"

"Ophelia. I've always liked the name." She placed Ophelia to her breast and helped guide the nipple into her mouth. "Come on and nurse, you precious little princess.

Otherwise, you'll be as skinny as your mother." She looked up with a teasing smile. "Or as skinny as Dr. Pearson."

"Don't worry, there's no way anybody can get that skinny." I smiled, but when I stood up my legs stiffened.

Fortunately, Angel gave me an excuse to take the time I needed. "Dr. Pearson, when should we restart the heparin?"

"We'll hold it, at least a day. We need to make sure you're not bleeding too much." I squatted to stretch my legs, holding to the bed for balance. "The most important thing was finding out you had protein S deficiency, the tendency to form a blood clot."

"That's why I was having one miscarriage after another?"

"Yep, and the main benefit of heparin is in allowing you to carry a pregnancy to term." Steady on my feet now, I stood straight. "You are at increased risk for a blood clot, though it's a small risk, so we'll restart the heparin soon. All the worry is over at this point. Ophelia's here."

I waved, grabbed my cane, and started for the door. "Try to get some rest, Angel, and I'll see you in a few hours."

"Thank you, Dr. Pearson, for everything."

I left the room, leaving the real work to Laverne, and lurched toward the nurse's station. I felt oddly detached, separated and sad. My right foot failed to lift and plowed into the carpet. I turned, pivoting on my left leg as I fell, and because I rolled toward my back, the crash was relatively safe. But the impact flung and scattered my cane, my stethoscope, my pens, and my pocket pharmacopoeia across the floor. The noise alerted Mary and Cerise and brought them running.

"Oh, Dr. Pearson, are you all right? Let me help you." Mary's Irish accent made me smile.

"No problem, no problem. I'm okay, just give me a second to get up." I couldn't jump up after a fall. To avoid the shakes and spasms associated with adrenaline, I needed to move slowly, calmly, but Mary and Cerise couldn't stand around while one of their doctors wallowed on the floor. Mary retrieved my pens and pharmacopoeia, and Cerise grabbed my stethoscope and cane before the two of them hoisted me to my feet. My legs shook but kept me upright.

"Thank you, thank you. You guys are wonderful, wonderful to help an eighty-year-old geezer like myself."

"Oh, Dr. Pearson, you're silly, but—oh, your elbow's bleeding. Let me get you some antiseptic and a Band-Aid."

I looked and shrugged. "It's just some rug burn, Mary. It's barely bleeding." I yelled after her, but she ignored me.

Cerise took the opportunity to examine my elbow and shook her head with a smile. "Maybe, you could wear elbow pads or something?"

"Yeah, or get myself some new legs."

When Mary returned with supplies, as she tended to my less than serious wound, she delivered a stern Irish-flavored admonition. "Oh, Dr. Pearson, you need to be careful. You've got a little scrape here. It looks pretty superficial, but still you have to be careful. You could really get hurt. It's carpet but it's hard. It's easy for anyone to fall down and break something. I knew a guy in Cork who thought—"

"It's okay, Mary. I'm fine. It's really no big deal. I fall all the time. I know how to fall. Honestly, I never, ever, ever get hurt. Not really, anyway."

I brushed myself off, smiled at Mary, and scowled at my cane. I was doing what I wanted to do, what I did well, even if my fingers trembled, my feet stumbled, and even if the carpet got streaked with a little red.

The phone jangled me awake – the clock read 4:17.

"Hello?"

"Dr. Pearson, it's Trevor. I'm taking care of Kai Paloma on the medical wing."

"Yeah, how's she doing?"

"I'm concerned. She woke up, and she's really confused, not making a lick of sense."

"Hold it. We're talking about Kai Paloma, the forty-seven-year-old woman in Room 119?"

"Correct. Her vitals are all stable, oxygen sat ninety-eight percent, but she's definitely confused."

"Shit!"

Falling

"Dr. Pearson?"

"Okay, let's add an ammonia level to the morning's labs, keep checking her stools for blood, start lactulose thirty cc three times a day, and make sure she doesn't hurt herself. I'll be there in thirty minutes."

I hung up the phone and staggered to my feet, quietly berating myself as I dressed. "You didn't want to give her diarrhea, but, damn it, you should have started lactulose."

Ursula rolled over, mumbling. "What dose? I don't know the dose." She was talking in her sleep.

"Nothing, nothing, just go back to sleep, Creature. Don't get up."

Twenty minutes later I was dressed, cane in hand, stethoscope around my neck, and opening the door into the garage when Denali cried. He sounded furious, as angry as a hornet, screaming at the cold wetness between his legs or the hollow in his belly or maybe both. I thought about going back but I knew I would fumble with diapers and formula, and the kids' room was a long way down the hall.

I heard Ursula stir, her sleepy voice clumsy with the Spanish words. "*Un momento, un momento,* Denali. I am certainly coming."

I felt cool air as I stepped into the garage, thankful that my job, despite its official description, was something less than full time.

But even part time can be deadly. More than twenty years before, working as a part-time medical assistant, Kai Paloma got hepatitis C from an inadvertent needle stick – a moment of inattention, a sudden turn or a tiny stumble, just enough to draw blood but not enough even for a Band-Aid. But that was all it took.

Slowly and inexorably, the hepatitis C virus had advanced, inflaming and then scarring Kai's liver until toxins like ammonia could no longer be eliminated, until many essential proteins could no longer be made, and until the liver all but surrendered. Now Kai was forty pounds heavier, slightly jaundiced, looking pregnant with a flabby belly and thick thighs that jiggled when she walked.

Yet, on admission, she had smiled like a child. I wondered now as I approached the nurse's station if I'd see her impish smile this morning.

"Nadine, how's Kai Paloma doing?"

"Her labs aren't back yet, but— hey, Dr. Pearson, what happened to your hand?" She was staring at the cast on my right hand.

"Oh, no big deal, I fell down and broke a couple metacarpals. I can still work. I just can't deliver any babies for a while. How's Kai?"

"She's wild. She won't drink the lactulose, and we're having a hard time keeping her in bed. Trevor and Andrea are in there now."

"Well, let me go see her, and then we'll get an NG tube down and probably transfer her to the unit."

Sure enough, Kai was wriggling and thrashing, pleading to her husband who wasn't even there. "I can't, Juan, I can't cook today. I'm too tired. Tired, tired. I can't. Are you listening?"

"Kai, it's Dr. Pearson. You're in the hospital. It's okay. We'll get you doing better."

"Juan, I don't want to go to the hospital. I don't need to go. Why won't you listen to me?"

"It's okay, Kai, just rest." I turned to Trevor. "Watch her, restrain her if necessary. I'll go write some orders to get her to the ICU."

Kai's labs printed out as I wrote the orders – all normal or not too abnormal, except for an ammonia level of 178. I frowned and shook my head. The nurses tried to ignore my grumbling. "Next time, Pearson, write for the damn lactulose."

I needn't have worried. There would be ample chance to get it right, for two days later, Kai was sitting up and smiling like a chubby elfin princess. "Hey, handsome, long time, no see. What'd you do to your hand?"

I put on a serious face. "You don't remember? You were flailing around, out of control, and you kicked me."

Kai sucked in a quick breath, her eyes and mouth open wide until I couldn't hold back my grin.

"Oooh, that's a good one. You crazy doctor, you had

me going there for a second." She fell back on the bed shaking
with laughter, clutching her chest. "I can see the headlines now.
Doctor Lies to Patient and She Has a Massive Heart Attack. You
had me going." She struggled to sit upright again. "But I'm so
silly; you already told me how you broke your hand."

"I see your memory's returning; that's good. Your
ammonia level and your weight are both down, so you should
be out of here soon, and that's exactly what I told the transplant
service down south."

"Good. They always want to know everything, but when
I see them, what do I say? I still don't know what happened."
The room grew quiet, and the mischievous grin was replaced by
a strained look and a trembling lip.

"You had a problem called encephalopathy, which
means your liver couldn't handle the toxins, such as ammonia,
and the ammonia built up in your blood until you were out of it.
We can treat the problem with lactulose, a liquid medicine, but
you were out of it and so we had to put it down the NG tube."
I pointed to the tube taped to Kai's nose. "Unfortunately, the
lactulose can give you some diarrhea and gas."

"Some! No kidding! I've been having nonstop diarrhea.
And gas, oh man, I let one loose earlier that should have
evacuated the hospital." She grinned ruefully and wagged a
finger at me. "Now I know who to blame."

"Unfortunately." I tried not to grin. "You're going to
need to be on lactulose from now on."

"Are you serious?"

"Yep, but we'll lower the dose. You'll also need higher
doses of the diuretics, the water pills."

"Great. I guess I'll live on the toilet, but can I at least get
this thing out of my nose?"

"No problem." I turned to Leslie who had just entered
the room with a syringe full of lactulose. "Let's take out the NG
tube and give the lactulose by mouth."

Without a word Leslie put on some gloves and moved to
withdraw the NG tube.

"Will this hurt?" Kai's gaze was piercing, willing me not
to joke.

"No, it won't," Leslie answered for me, and took out the NG tube with a rapid pull.

"Oh, ouch!" Kai was touching her nose, gingerly. "That wasn't as bad as I thought, but you hospital people are good at torturing us poor patients."

Before she left the room Leslie smiled at Kai. "Just be thankful you don't remember me putting it in."

"No kidding." Kai let go of her nose. "Can you tell Juan about all this, the lactulose, ammonia, and water pills? My silly hubby's not handling my illness very well. He's going out a lot, angry all the time. He thinks I'm being lazy."

Her eyes misted up, but she shook her head. "I guess now I'll be Juan's perfect girl, lazy, fat, and farting all day. I can see it now, 'I didn't have the time to make dinner or do the laundry, honey, but I did manage to stink up the house real good.'"

She started to laugh, but I wanted to get the facts before any potential tears could appear. "Is Juan hitting you?"

"No." She seemed to find the question, like most everything else, humorous. "I can't even imagine such a thing."

"Does he have a girlfriend on the side?"

"He better not! Or I'll have to hit him good." Kai started to shake her head, then said, "Honestly, I don't think he has a girlfriend."

Leslie was back with a cup of orange liquid that she handed to Kai.

"Well, maybe, he's just having a hard time dealing with your health problems. One way people sometimes try to cope is by distancing themselves from the partner who's ill. I'd give him some time, but keep trying to talk to him. He may come around. It's always hardest on the loved ones."

Kai looked down at the cup, at the orange-amber liquid, mostly clear but too bright and sweet to pass for iced tea. "Are you sure about that?"

"Yep, always."

Kai tilted her head as if to get a better look at me, then lifted the plastic cup as if it were a toast in Dom Perignon. "Well, here's to always."

Falling

A cold bottle can't replace a warm breast, and Ophelia must have fussed more often than not on the day that her mother, Angel, disappeared. I'm sure that Cheryl, Angel's own mother, did her best. She seemed to understand babies – cries swiftly answered and pain promptly soothed. It was the older kids she complained about, the teenagers with their foul language and restless ways, their focus, not on school or church, but on their own internal sensations, as if an orgasm or a drug high would or could do anything but fade.

Cheryl had raised her daughter the right way, her way, with family and discipline, church and love, and her daughter had almost always used correct language. So it mystified Cheryl now how her beautiful, beloved, white-gowned daughter had managed to tiptoe down life's muddiest path only to trip and fall headfirst into the swamp. And she'd taken the plunge into drugs not once but twice. Living clean must not have been enough.

By all accounts, Cheryl looked everywhere for Angel, repeatedly driving around the seedy parts of our town, the docks, and even the hard-to-reach hangouts. Some people had to see the pain in Cheryl's eyes, and maybe they even knew where women like Angel were to be found. But no one gave her away. At the local health center, nobody knew where Angel was either, but there were rumors. It was always a friend of a friend of someone who knew a woman who shot crank or smoked crack, but the description was vague and didn't seem to match.

Ophelia was about four months old when word got around that Angel was back in town – if she'd ever even left. When I heard that Angel was staying with another of my drug-abusing patients, I insisted that somebody bring her to clinic right away. I even entertained a fleeting notion of canceling clinic altogether so I could go to find her, to help her, as if I had some magic formula that could wipe all her troubles and shame away.

I was eating lunch when Angel arrived, so I didn't see her enter an exam room. I didn't see the medical assistants taking her vitals, didn't see their heads shaking, their looks, and even when I lurched into the room a little later, cane in hand, stethoscope at the ready, the Angel I saw was not the Angel I knew. Stringy hair, dirty clothes, that much I expected. But her formerly bright, clear face was now drawn, her skin peeling, a mass of pimples and oozing sores over skeletal bones. She saw me, then took in my expression and began to weep into her hands. I couldn't keep looking at her, it was too painful as I tried to control my own emotions. Then I looked at the chart – eighty-three pounds.

"Eighty-three pounds! Damn it. Eighty-three pounds."

Angel kept crying, and I looked everywhere but at her to try to regain some control. I wanted to scream at her, shake her, slap her, anything to make her see reality. Anything to bring back the Angel who'd always kept her appointments and faithfully injected her medicine, the woman loved by the obstetric nurses, the Angel who apologized for saying "Shit" and didn't want to push even though the baby's head was right there.

I sucked air through clenched teeth. "Damn it, Angel, what about your daughter? What about Ophelia?"

Angel lifted her head, her eyes half-closed. "She's with my mom, Dr. Pearson. She's all right. I— " Then she choked up and hid her face in her hands again.

"That's not what I meant."

Had she nodded off? No, she soon responded. "I know, I know."

It was all I could do to keep the conversation going, my voice cracking with emotion. "Angel, we have to get you into a treatment program. You have to stop, or you're going to die."

"I know. It's my own fault. My mom's trying to find a program for me. She wants me to move in with her. She wants to help me." She raised her grimy, tear-streaked face and sucked her bottom lip. "But I'm the one who has to do it. I'm the only one who can do it."

"You can do it, Angel. You can do it. What are you on?"

"Speed, methamphetamines." She paused, panting as if exhausted. "I'm injecting it." She said it as if she barely believed it herself.

"Are you sharing needles? There's a lot of hepatitis C around here."

"I have plenty of needles. I've been hoarding them. I've never shared." That one tiny thread of hope lasted only seconds. "I haven't been injecting heparin like I should." She looked down at her hands and began to sob.

"Angel, listen to me. Have you been trading sex for drugs? Do we need to worry about sexually transmitted diseases?"

"No, I haven't done that. Never."

I didn't know whether to believe her, but I ordered the necessary tests anyway. At the moment I couldn't imagine anyone, not even a hard-up junkie, wanting sex with the sore-ridden, smelly near-corpse in front of me.

"Angel, I know the meth gives you an incredible rush, but, please, think of your mom, think of Ophelia. Think of yourself. You weigh just eighty-three pounds. Haven't you had enough? Aren't you ready to get clean?"

She raised her head and looked directly at me, her eyes no longer awash in tears. "I am —" The effort seemed too much for her. She swallowed and tried again. "I am not going to —" After that she just lowered her head and shook it in a silent no.

"It's okay, Angel. Just rest. We'll get you some food. We'll get you some help. You haven't shared needles or traded sex for drugs. That's good. All we have to do is get you off the meth." I said it like it was simple, easy, like watching less television or eating fewer Big Macs.

But Angel didn't smile or even look up. She knew it wasn't easy at all.

"Let me step out and have the nurse and social worker start work on getting you into a program. We'll work with your mom. It would be harder if you didn't have money, but since your mom will pay for it, we should be able to get you in. It's going to be okay. I'll give you my number. Please, please, call me anytime." I reached across and gave her a hug, but I felt more bones than hope.

When Angel left the clinic a short time later after urinating in a cup and having blood drawn, she shuffled as if sleepwalking, and she never went back to her friend's house. After that nobody saw her on the streets of our town or any neighboring ones, and even the rumors didn't flare.

A week later a drug treatment program in a nearby town had an opening for Angel, but after three failed attempts to reach her they had to let the spot go to some other addict, probably one just as desperate but not as polite.

"My belly and feet are all swollen." Kai lay in the hospital bed, clutching her wide belly and wriggling her toes. "And I've been taking all the medicine, and I haven't been eating that much."

"Oh, man, you're puffy." I was busy pressing on her ankles.

"Except for that cheesecake at Aunt Kelsie's. It was so good I just couldn't help myself."

"Have you been having belly pain or fevers?"

"No, but I expected some pain after eating so much."

"Kai, this is not from eating cheesecake." I shook my head. "Your water pills aren't doing the job."

Her eyes widened. "So do I keep getting bigger and bigger until I blow up?"

"Well, let's add a third water pill called Diamox. There's one study that found it to work well with Lasix and Aldactone. Hopefully, it'll shrink you. Let's give it a day. I'll admit you, but, maybe you can go home tomorrow." I started toward the door with my walker, anticipating a long day in clinic.

"Okay, you're the doctor, but hold it a second. You're not getting away that easy. I want the inside scoop. What's that?" She pointed to my walker. "Are you making a fashion statement, or have you finally decided to stop falling down?"

I felt my face grow warm. "Yeah, it works pretty well and keeps me upright, but it's a little bulky, like driving a Hummer."

"I must say I'll miss your creative attempts to keep from falling, but I like this walker. It's rather chic."

"Yeah, in a crippled sort of way."

It wasn't that funny, but Kai's laughter gave me a lift. On my way out the door I smiled and kept smiling, even after I got drenched in the rain on the way to my car, even after my walker's brakes broke halfway through clinic. The next day Kai's weight was down, her belly not so protuberant, and Juan took her back to their tiny hometown.

Over the next ten months, though, the hospital became Kai's second home – eight admissions, four for swelling, two for vomiting, one for anemia, and one for mild confusion after Kai secretly lowered her dose of lactulose. Eight times I probed her with questions and lights and fingers, eight times she wiggled on the gurney, laughing at her belly, her feet, and her flab. Eight times I called the transplant service downstate, explaining, reassuring, and trying to sound confident, competent.

Then one day Kai came to clinic with a new problem.

"I can't seem to catch my breath. I go to the kitchen and I'm huffing and puffing. I go to the bathroom and I'm huffing and puffing. I just can't get enough air."

"How long's this been going on?" I was already writing admission orders in my mind.

"About a week, but it's gotten bad the last couple days."

"Any cough?"

"No."

"Fevers?"

"No."

"Black stools?"

"No"

"Vomiting?"

"No."

"Chest pain?"

"No."

"Night sweats?"

"No, no, no. There's absolutely nothing else wrong. I'm fine when I'm sitting, but when I move or talk too much, I just can't catch my breath." She stared at me waiting for an answer.

I stared back, finally saying, "I don't know."

For some reason my answer tickled us both, and we began to laugh.

"But you're the doctor. You're supposed to know. You're supposed to say something like, 'It's huff-and-puff syndrome, very common with hepatitis C. Don't worry, Kai. We see it all the time.' "

"I think I skipped that lecture in medical school."

"Oh, great!" She rolled her eyes to tease me. "I've either got a slacker for a doctor or a comedian."

I was still chuckling as I placed my stethoscope on her back, moved it here and there, told her to breathe, told her not to breathe. After ten minutes I still didn't know. I took the ends of the tubes out of my ears and hung the stethoscope around my neck. "I'm not sure what's going on. I think your breath sounds are a little diminished on the left, but we'll get an x-ray to check it out. Could you have pneumonia? I doubt it. Could you have fluid below your lung? Maybe, but your oxygen saturation's not too bad. Could you be more anemic than usual? Maybe. Could you have some strange heart problem? I doubt it. Let's get you up to our hospital and go from there."

"Are you serious?"

"I'm serious, Kai. We need to find out what's wrong, and I can't do it in this little clinic on a Friday."

"Okay, I'll go in for the zillionth time." She sighed and shook her head. "But I don't want any mean nurses or nurses who go on three-hour breaks, and I don't want any young and pretty, plastic-fantastic nurses, no way. Juan will spend all day staring and drooling, and he won't even notice me." At that her eyes seemed to dance with mischief. "You need to get me either an old but nice-as-pie female nurse, or a young, handsome male nurse with a good body and a thing for full-figured women."

"Don't worry. I'll write the order just the way you say."

That evening the asymmetry of Kai's chest x-ray could be seen from across the room. A large white area extended halfway up the left side, ending at a perfectly horizontal line. Above the line, the left lung fought to retain its air, and even though gravity was helping, the suffocating flow seeped ever upward, pushing the boundary.

"Kai, you've got a large amount of fluid beneath your left lung. We may need to drain it with a needle."

"What? Fluid? What kind of fluid? How'd it get there?" She blinked with the questions.

"It's called a pleural effusion, and a lot of things could

cause it, but most likely it's from your liver not doing so well. I'll increase your water pills to the maximum, but it probably won't get the fluid off your lung. You'll probably need a procedure called a thoracentesis where we put a needle in your back to draw out the fluid. It's pretty safe, and the radiologist does it with an ultrasound to make sure he hits the right spot. We can probably schedule it for the morning."

"Stop. Hold it. Time out." Kai's eyes darted toward the door before fluttering and then settling on me. "All right, all right – you're my doctor, you know my case better than anyone – if you say it's necessary, then—" She nodded.

"It is, but it's not just me. I spoke with the transplant team this morning, and they agree. It's not as big a deal as you might think. Sometimes patients can have a thoracentesis on an outpatient basis. They come in, get the fluid taken off, and go home an hour or so later."

"Okay, explain to me again the benefits of doing this?"

"First, we can find out if there's an infection or some other problem that's causing the fluid to build up – in your case it's probably your liver. Second, you'll breathe a lot better once we get that fluid off your lung."

"Good. I'm tired of running a marathon every time I make dinner for Juan."

"Speaking of your hubby, how are things going between you two?"

"Much, much better. At first, he didn't want to believe I was sick. He actually accused me of faking it." She paused to make a fist, suck some air, and laugh. "When he finally got it through his thick skull that I was sick, he just knew I was going to die at any moment. I couldn't even use the toilet without him asking if I was okay. Every time I so much as belched, he wanted me to call you." She shook her head, grinning. "But now he's better. He knows there's a problem, but he isn't freaking out."

We sat in silence together for a bit, then she spotted my walker.

"So how's Ursula dealing with your health problems?"

"Ursh? Oh, she's great. Luckily, my problems have developed slowly, and so we've both had time to adjust, but

it puts a strain on her. Between the twins and me, she's got
her hands full. I play with the twins, but as for helping her
with work, I can't help much, partly because I'm always in
the hospital, partly because I have physical limitations, partly
because I'm just plain lazy."

I was already pushing my walker toward the door. "I'll
see you first thing in the morning, before the thoracentesis."

Sometimes, at night when nobody is watching, the fluid
level drops, the effusion drains, and nobody knows why — not
doctors or patients or preachers. Next morning there's little trace
of what was there the day before, except for a faint line that
marks the vanished border where a battle had raged.

I made my laborious way to Kai's room where her
husband was sitting with her. "Kai, I've got good news. Your
water pills have kicked in. I just looked at your chest x-ray, and
the effusion is gone, completely gone."

"Are you saying what I think?"

"Yep, there's no need for a thoracentesis, at least not this
time."

"Far out! Can I go home?"

" You bet." I smiled as I looked over Kai's breakfast tray.
"You'll have to go home soon, but don't worry, you'll have the
opportunity to sample our scrumptious scrambled eggs along
with our fruit cup featuring fresh melons from the south side of,
um, Peru."

Kai stabbed the melon with her fork. "Definitely Peru."

"But unfortunately you'll have to check out of our hotel
after breakfast."

"Oh darn, and I so wanted to try the fried-oyster
surprise at lunch." Kai laughed and turned to Juan. "You
hear that, honey? We'll be out early, enough time to do a little
shopping and maybe even hang out at the beach."

Juan looked doubtful. "Okay, if you say so, but don't get
us into trouble by feeding the seagulls."

"Oh, just a little. They're always so hungry." Kai took a
bite of her scrambled eggs. "I love to sit on the beach and throw
bread crumbs to the birds. They come right up to you squawking
and flapping, as if to say 'Give it to me. I need it. I'm the one,

right here.' So I throw them breadcrumbs and make sure they all get a mouthful, not just the biggest and most aggressive. Then when the bread's all gone. I like to sit back and relax, watch the waves and sky, and wonder what year it is."

"What year it is?" I didn't follow.

Kai nodded. "The ocean and the sky must have looked the same a hundred years ago, the same clouds, the same foamy water. And I bet the waves will still crash the same a hundred years into the future, the same sounds, the same sand. So, you see, sometimes it's easy to forget the year."

"Okay, I'll do my part in helping you forget by getting you out of here." I lurched toward the door, pushing my walker ahead. "Let's hope we can keep you out of the hotel for a while."

It was a Saturday morning nine days later while I was tussling with and tickling Denali and Jasmine that the phone rang. When I reached for it, the two toddler commandos used the opportunity to yell and escape down the hall.

"Hello?"

"It's me again. I'm huffing and puffing, worse than ever, but there's nothing else wrong."

"Have you been taking your meds?"

"Yes. Should I take more?"

"It won't help. You're already on the maximum dose of Lasix, Aldactone, and Diamox. You probably need a thoracentesis."

"Okay, but can I do it and go home afterwards?"

Suddenly, the miniature commandos were back, screaming and running and brandishing their blankets. "Hold on, Kai." I lowered the receiver. "You guys need to hold on just a second. Daddy has to talk on the phone, and it's important."

"Sick people?"

"Yes, Jasmine, it's the sick people."

With that, she whispered something to Denali, and they ran back down the hall.

"Sorry. Where were we?"

"Was that your daughter?"

"Yep, that was Jasmine, a.k.a. 'Super Bear.' "

"How old is she?"

"A rambunctious two, but let's shift gears. You need to go to the hospital for a chest x-ray right now. I'll call in the order, and I'll call Dr. Cerra and see if he can do the thoracentesis this morning."

"Then I get to go home?"

"Maybe, if he can do it today. Otherwise, you'll have to be admitted. Either way I'll meet you in the x-ray department in about an hour."

"Why do you have to come? The other doctor will do the thora-thing-a-ma-jig, and it's Saturday. Why don't you stay home and play with your kids? There's no sense in coming to the hospital if you don't have to?"

"Maybe you're right. The thoracentesis is pretty straightforward, and you'll like Dr. Cerra."

"See, nothing for you to do."

"Maybe, but if there's a problem, I'll come down. The important thing is for you to get yourself to the hospital now."

"Juan's here. We're leaving as soon as I get off the phone."

"Okay, but if there are any problems I'll come down."

There were no problems on that Saturday. Dr. Cerra graciously agreed to perform the thoracentesis. He removed one and a half liters from Kai's left lung, and studies showed that the fluid was not infected.

Yet sometimes, even though the right things are done at the right times, even though the patient smiles and coughs, sucking air anew, and even though the beaches are sunny and sandy and full of life, time cannot be forgotten. The gulls might swoop and scream along the shoreline, stealing what scraps they can get, but the tide is rising, and soon all will be underwater, and everyone will know not only the year but the very hour.

Tuesday morning the fluid was back. I admitted Kai to the hospital for a repeat thoracentesis, then called the transplant center. The physicians there wanted time to discuss the case and told me to expect a call soon. Several calls did interrupt my clinic that day, but not the one I hoped for. At day's end, thoughts of Kai followed me home. And for once it wasn't my fault.

Ursula

"Might Kai eat chicken curry?"

"What?" Clint was watching television, slow to change his focus.

"You know, Kai, your patient. Can she have chicken curry, or is she simply too sick?"

"She can have it as long as she doesn't eat a ton of chicken, but she probably doesn't even like curry."

"But she does like it. She said as much, and I promised I'd bring her some tomorrow at brunch."

"When did you talk—?"

"Clint, might I offer you a wake-up call? I speak with her on the tele. She calls almost every week. I spoke with her today for almost an hour." I smiled, shaking my head.

"Sorry, I guess—" He shrugged, appropriately repentant, so I didn't belabor the point.

"If I may ask, what is the plan for her? Might she finally be going to the transplant center for a new liver?"

"I don't know. I spoke with them and did my best, but they seemed reluctant to take her. Her synthetic liver functions aren't terribly bad, and she's had no recurrent GI bleeds. She just keeps getting this damned pleural effusion and—"

"The fluid on her lungs?"

"Yeah, fluid on her lungs. Finally I told them that I'm out of tricks and open to suggestions. At first they said more diuretics, more water pills, but after I told them what she was on, they just said they'd run the case by the hepatologists and get back to me. I don't know." He shook his head.

"Did you ever seek to transfer her before? In all the times you had her in the hospital, did you ever seek a transfer until now?" My face felt very warm, and I found myself clenching my teeth as I spoke. "Bloody doctors."

Clint

The next morning Kai pelted me with questions.
"Am I going to the trasnplant center? Do I go after another
thoracentesis? Do they know everything that's happening? What
did you say to them? What are they waiting for? Don't they get
it?"

I did my best to answer her and urged patience. But
many of Kai's questions were also my own, and after reaching
the clinic, I slammed the car door so hard I nearly fell.

Clinic was relatively uneventful: a cancelled
appointment, two Pap smears, three diabetic checks, and a
pneumonia follow-up. Just before lunch my medical assistant
opened the door to tell me that a nurse from the local hospital
was on the phone.

"Dr. Pearson, it's Francine. The transplant center wants
Kai. You need to come back and write the transfer order. I can't
take a verbal order for a transfer."

"That's great! I can't believe it."

"I know. She was in her room with her husband when
the news came. They got all excited, hollering and crying. Are
you going to be able to?"

"I'll be there in twenty minutes."

Francine rushed the chart to me as soon as I entered the
hospital. "I thought I'd save you some steps. Kai's over in x-ray,
getting a thoracentesis, and I didn't want you to have to run all
over."

"Thanks." I spun my walker around and sat down on its
seat. "It's not easy driving this Hummer around the hospital."

"Here's the transfer packet. I filled out most of it. All you
have to do is sign."

"Beautiful." I signed and grinned, feeling like I had won
the lottery. "I can't believe it."

Francine asked the crucial question. "Do you think she'll
really get a liver?"

"She still has several hurdles. Most people die while
waiting for a liver, but she's cleared the first hurdle, and I have

a gut feeling she'll be okay." I stood and spun my walker to walking position. My legs shook as if I had been sitting for hours.

"Dr. Pearson, are you going over to x-ray?"

"I better not. I have to get back, and, besides, if I go over there now, I'll get all emotional and embarrass myself. I'll see her much later." I looked down the hall to calm myself. "I'll see her when she comes back with a new liver." Then I smiled, waved at Francine, and danced my walker toward the exit.

On the way to clinic, however, my elation melted like warm ice cream. In my mind, I reviewed Kai's hospitalizations, trying to see if something had been missed: the medicines ordered, allergies noted, potassium checked, cultures taken, notes dictated. Then, amid the details of my medical fretting, there came an odd thought. Had Kai had the chance to try Ursula's curry? Did she find it too spicy, or did she like it? I knew Ursh would ask.

Before reaching the clinic, I took a brief detour along the river to the ocean where I parked the car to eat my lunch. A small family sat at a picnic table, enjoying the sunshine. The parents were talking as their young daughter munched on French fries and ketchup. Two seagulls watched the child, now and then hopping closer, just not close enough to steal any food. Down by the water a woman was taking photographs. After I rolled down my window, the sound of water caught my attention and made me look deeper than I wanted.

Where it poured into the ocean, the river ran rushing and powerful, but the stronger ocean swallowed it in waves and swells and spray. The motion was violent but continual, strangely sleepy. Nothing, not pieces of weathered driftwood or tender broadleaf or a forgotten running shoe, could escape the flow.

Yet, foam seemed to try. It gathered, loitering near the banks of the river, as if hoping to stall, hiding behind rocks or within momentary eddies, anything to postpone the inevitable embrace and weight of the ocean. It seemed everyone and everything was like that, streaming toward the sea, unable to stop, flailing and sputtering and spitting, at least, until the sea lifted and covered all, washing in the sickening taste of brine.

Although clinic didn't start for fifteen minutes, on this day the rush of the river was simply too strong and the scent of salt too close. I packed up my lunch, started the car, and drove away.

The phone jangled me awake from a dreamless sleep. The clock read "1:03," as I slid the receiver in the general direction of my ear.

"Dr. Pearson here."

"This is Dr. Reynolds at the transplant center. Sorry to call you so late, but I'm taking care of Kai Paloma. She coded, and the family insisted that I call you."

"Coded? What happened?"

"She was found unresponsive. She's now intubated and requiring blood pressure support with both dopamine and Levophed."

"Oh, no." I remembered how the ICU nurses used to joke that the correct name for Levophed was "Leave-'em-dead."

"We don't know how long she was down. It appears she's had a massive GI bleed."

"What's her pressure on dopamine and Levophed?"

"Almost nothing, sixty-five over thirty, and she's requiring hundred percent oxygen on a nonrebreather to maintain seventy percent sats."

"Oh, no, no." I squeezed the receiver, resisting the urge to pound it against the nightstand. Ursula awakened and looked at me.

"Sorry to give you bad news and to call you so late. I'll keep you posted."

"Thanks." I put down the phone.

"Is it Kai?"

"Yeah, she coded, has a GI bleed, and fuck." I shook my head, biting my lower lip. "She's not going to make it. No chance, no chance in hell. Goddamn it."

"Shame." I could sense Ursh studying my face in the dark. "Are you okay?"

"Yeah, I'm all right." I was surprised that the words and tone sounded true. "I won't be able to sleep, but I'm okay. I'll go watch some TV. Go to sleep, Creature."

"Shame." Ursh sighed and snuggled into the blankets. "Don't stay up too late."

Too stiff to walk, I used my walker to hop out the door and down the hallway.

At first in the living room I couldn't find the remote control and mumbled a few "fucks" and "goddamns" before I saw it atop the television. I settled for a movie I'd seen before, *Blade Runner*, and although the first time around I'd found it suspenseful, poignant, and dark, now I was wondering how old Harrison Ford and Darryl Hannah were when they made the film. Then I thought about their current lives and loves – as if I actually knew them – recalling their movies and their reported tabloid shenanigans. Soon tired of meaningless conjecture, I turned off the television and went back to bed.

The next morning I noticed something different — an unusual background hum or drone. Sometimes it was buzzing like a horsefly or just whining near my ear like a mosquito. Sometimes, it was softer, less intrusive, like a radio left on in the back room. Ursula didn't hear it, but there it was, all the time, when I combed my hair, when I put on my socks, when I entered the hospital, and when I stumbled toward my car at the end of the day.

A week later, two weeks before Christmas, the noise followed me to the clinic and continued to whir nonstop as I saw patients. It murmured unintelligibly in my ear while I examined the scabies and scratches of Melody Stanford's children. It droned and even seemed to purr while I listened to the wheeze in Dan Floyd's lungs. And it became vacuous and hypnotic, like the sound inside a conch shell, while I counseled Sheila Morris about hepatitis C treatment. By the end of clinic, the constant hum had become unsettling, as if I had forgotten something in the rush and motion of daily life.

I drove toward home in the dark. My stomach growled, and my cell phone rang, reminding me that I was on call. Of course, crap.

"Dr. Pearson here"

"Clint, it's George Isler in the E.R. I've got a patient of yours, a Mr. Tyrus Burns."

"Yeah, I know him well." A train wreck.

"He's a fifty-one-year-old alcoholic with diabetes, hypertension, COPD, and coronary-artery disease who was assaulted and found down in town and brought in by ambulance. He has multiple abrasions on his face, an open fracture of his right arm, and is very intoxicated. The CT scan of his head is negative for a bleed, and I've already called ortho, but given his many medical problems, you'll need to be involved."

"I'm driving back from clinic now, and I should be there in about twenty minutes." I clicked off the phone. So much for dinner.

I turned on the radio hoping to overrule the buzz in my head. Reception was good, and Nellie Furtado was singing with her distinctive and sensual vibrato, slow and soft and a little plaintive. Before long I began to sing with her. "Your faith in me brings me to tears, even after—"

The road turned and the song drowned in a wave of static. Shit, goddamn radio. A few curves would have brought reception back in a minute or so, but I snapped off the radio and drove on in a quiet both droning and uneasy.

Twenty minutes later, I parked my car at the hospital, in front of two smiling but unkempt guys standing out on the sidewalk to smoke. They looked up, pointed toward the night sky as if identifying some celestial formation. With no time for stargazing, I staggered to the back of my car to unload my walker.

"Hey, buddy, you need a hand?" The astronomers had obviously witnessed my lurch-and-grab along the side of the car.

"No thanks. I got it. No problem." I opened the hatch, heaved my walker out, and slammed the door with a grunt. A breeze let me know the guys were smoking more than tobacco, but I didn't bother to smile.

A few steps from the entrance, I was startled by a shrill cry, a flapping sound, and a sudden plop on my pants leg. I didn't bother to look up, for I knew immediately what had happened.

"Hey, buddy, did that little fucker get you?"

I waved him away. "Yeah, but I'll wash it off inside." If I ever get two seconds of fucking free time.

What else? What else does this damn night have to offer? With short, stiff steps, I staggered inside where I saw a shiny white stain on my pants. Just great.

My face felt flushed, but before I could think about rest, my pager blared out a call from the answering service. Now what? Somebody wants to know the proper dose of Tylenol? As I shook my head, the irritating hum sounded ever closer, louder.

Only ten feet away from the front desk phone, I figured the waiting room's tile floor harbored no troublesome rugs or cords, but it didn't matter. I could barely lift my feet to walk, and as I struggled I could feel hot pity on the back of my neck from those waiting to be seen. Fuck you. I'm a doctor.

At the desk, I managed to spin my walker around and sit down, but before I could wipe my face and reach for the phone, my pager beeped again with the same sequence of flashing numbers. Chill out, assholes. I'm answering as fast as I can.

"Dr. Pearson here."

"Yes, Dr. Pearson, we have a call from Marilyn Pollier. She called about Jason Pollier, her two-year-old son, who has a stiff neck, a headache, and is running a fever of a hundred and three. The number is 458-2323."

Holy shit, why doesn't she take the kid to the E.R.? I dialed the number, and as I waited through the intermittent rings, I felt a feather-light tap on my right shoulder. It was so light that I dismissed it as an accidental touch from someone. But then it recurred, less tentative than before, then I felt it again and again.

I shook my head, hunkered down, and waved off the intrusion. Give me a second, damn it, give me just one second! Can't you see that I'm answering an urgent call, that this child could die, that I have an admission waiting for me in the E.R., that I'm hungry, that the radio in my head can't find the fucking station and won't turn off, that I'm sweating in December, and for crying out loud, you damn-near blind, shoulder-tapping bastard, can't you, at least, see and appreciate the smear of pearly birdshit on my pants leg?

I was standing, a little unsteadily, leaning against a tall cedar on the mountainside less than halfway up Dennison Peak. In each hand, I held a cane but didn't walk, just stood, and stared downward. My camouflage pants were worn thin, starting to fray along the seams. The waistline fit but only with my belt's help. My right pants leg was speckled with dark smudges of leaf mold plus the previous day's chocolate pudding.

A cool breeze raced up the mountain, rustling through the pines and making a bluejay squawk, but otherwise all was quiet. Even though it was almost midday, the cloud cover was dense enough to dampen the sun. I stared downward, grumbled, and spat to land near a lone ant. The ant darted swiftly back and forth amidst the pine needles and decaying buckeyes. I examined my forearms, studying the patterns of scratches, blood, and dirt, then my T-shirt, to the Nike emblem and slogan, "There is no finish line."

After a deep breath, I raised my head to survey the mountain. I thought the summit was visible, seemingly reachable, above rock outcroppings. To my left, a growth of cedar and scrub pine looked like an easier climb among the rocks.

I started that way, canes testing and feet trying to overcome the incline. At first I managed to stay upright and shuffle forward twenty feet or so until the slope grew steeper. Then, no matter what strategy I tried — twisting, kicking, or crouching — my feet just would not make the grade. In frustration, I growled deep in my throat, then flung both canes to the ground and clawed at the rocks, roots, and dirt on hands and knees. Using my elbows to wedge, my knees to balance, and my hands to pull, I willed myself upward an inch at a time. My face burned, but my progress was so slow that most ten-year-olds could have made it in half the time.

I persisted until I reached the base of the rocks. There I rested, shaking my arms and surveying the damage. With red, oozing elbows and fresh scrapes and scratches crisscrossing my hands and forearms, I clasped hands over my knees and whispered encouragement to myself. "Come on, hang in there, you're doing good."

After fifteen minutes of rest I tried to grab the rock and hoist myself upright, but it didn't happen. I was stuck in a sort of question-mark stance before I fell back to the ground. With a scowl and a sigh, I shifted and sat up to survey the land below me.

Scraggly pines and scattered rock formations marked the ridges above a sea of black oak, juniper, and manzanita closer to Jack Flats Campground. Compared to my usual route up Dennison, the landscape here was safer, warmer, drier, with no rocky gorges or waterfalls.

As I sat I shook my head slowly and emphatically from side to side. I grabbed the rock and with shuddering legs finally managed to stand. When a red ant emerged from a crack and scurried about, thoughtlessly I smacked the ant and brushed the tiny, gyrating body off the rock. At that I teetered again, then steadied myself with a hand to the rock. I shook my head. "Don't be a fool, fall on your ass just to kill an ant."

A light sprinkle of rain suddenly began but stopped almost immediately. I nodded and gazed upward to study the route. An inviting crack ran for forty or fifty feet along the rock, at a far less than vertical pitch. It would do. I restarted my climb.

Like an inept, inexperienced climber, I relied on my arms so that my legs dangled beneath me, contributing little. Even so, I rose steadily, straining and grunting with each new move. After twenty minutes, I reached the middle of the rock, when a bluejay suddenly squawked and went on squawking. Then the crack narrowed, encrusted with a dry lichen that rubbed off in dusty flakes. I advanced a couple more feet before my arms gave out.

"Oh, shit, not now."

I squirmed and tried to kick my right foot into a small fissure, but my boot thumped uselessly against the rock. I started to pant, scanning the rock for handholds. Three feet above me, a small but seemingly sturdy pine jutted out, so I studied it as I tried to rest, but my left hand slid a little, and my face flooded with warmth as I re-gripped.

"Fuck you, I'm gonna make it."

I shifted, growling, straining to lift my right leg. When that knee scraped the rock, the whole leg jerked suddenly upward and would have pulled me from the rock had my right boot not stuck in a crease.

Stable for the moment, I knew I couldn't stay that way for long. I glanced again at the tree, took two quick breaths, and launched myself up and out. Well, sort of. My legs did no more than extend, and by the time gravity took hold, my fingers were sliding on rock like rain on dusty slate.

CHAPTER FIFTEEN

Hope

It's nice when grown people whisper to each
other under the covers.
Their ecstasy is more leaf-sigh than bray and
the body is the vehicle,
not the point.
-- from Toni Morrison's *Jazz*

Ursula

Clint only received minor injuries in his final attempt to
climb Dennison years ago, and now he's accepted that he can no
longer climb. In fact he's been going to work in a power-chair for
the past three years. So we decided to revisit the mountains in
a safe manner, by driving our van to Blue Ridge, close to where
Clint used to climb.

Near the summit, I had no more than stopped the van
when Clint raced out in his power-chair, followed by our now
six-year-old twins. After ten minutes or so of tidying our van, I
followed only to stop to catch my breath in the thin mountain
air. I shaded my eyes with my hand and looked for Clint and the
kids.

At the top of the ridge and some distance above me,
Clint sat in his power-chair, while Jasmine sought to capture his
attention.

Clint

When Jasmine tapped and pulled on my shoulder, I was harkened back to a trying day four years before.

I was in the lobby of our local emergency room. Patients waited, some clamoring to be seen. A telephone rang and rang, a sick child was crying somewhere too far away for anyone to hear. And someone with no sense at all wouldn't stop tapping my shoulder. I turned to see a robust, healthy face and a smile.

"Angel! Angel, oh my God, you look great, beautiful!" I managed to stand.

"Thank you, Dr. Pearson." She blushed. "I'm clean now, and I'm sorry I gave you and everyone else such a hard time."

I grinned, shaking my head. "The only one you gave a hard time to was yourself, but it doesn't matter now. You did it, you're back, and you look great. But— "

"Would you like to see Ophelia? She's right over here." She pointed to a nearby chair where a toddler slept amidst pillows.

"Oh, she looks so big." I walked over to her while Angel answered my unspoken questions.

"I knew I had to stop the drugs and get Ophelia back, and I knew my only chance was to leave the area and get away from all the temptations. I moved to Idaho and lived in a shelter there. A month later, my mom brought up Ophelia. I admit I was tempted a couple of times, but ooh—" Her jaw clenched at the memory. "I just wasn't going to lose Ophelia again. She needs and deserves a mommy, not some stupid, strung- out—" She shook her head, then glanced at my walker. "But how have you been, Dr. Pearson?"

"Oh, about the same, hanging in there and seeing patients, but what brings you here? Is Ophelia sick?"

"Yes, she has a cold, and I want to get her checked out. I'm sorry but I can't go to the clinic any more. There are too many people I know there, people on drugs. It's too much of a temptation for me."

"Don't worry about it. All that matters is that you stay clean and that you and Ophelia stay well." Feeling my emotions starting to rise, I bit my lower lip and looked away. "I've got a patient waiting for me, so I have to run, but seeing you two now is the best Christmas present I could possibly have."

When we hugged, I had to keep one hand on my walker for balance. But afterward, as I shuffled toward the E.R., my legs started to lift and stride. At the entrance a patient held the door, and I smiled, nodded my thanks, and danced through, humming an almost forgotten song.

"Daddy, Denali won't listen to me or Mom. He went climbing on those rocks."

I smiled at her precocious zeal. "Since when do you listen to Mom?"

She stomped but looked about and changed the subject. "So what's this mountain called again?"

"Blue Ridge. The mountain across the canyon is Homer's Nose, and the one to the right is Dennison. I used to climb them both."

"Yeah, and Mom says you almost killed yourself on Dennison."

"I got a few scratches but—"

"Hey, what are you guys doing?" Before we could answer, Denali bounded over a rock to us.

"Just hanging out. Is Mom coming?"

"Yeah." Denali sat down on a boulder. "She's always got one more thing to do."

"Like picking up your stuff?"

Denali frowned at the question and posed one of his own. "Why'd you drive off the road?"

"No reason, just checking things out and remembering when I used to climb."

I picked up a rock and casually tossed it down the mountain. It landed, bounced, and went on tumbling in a miniature landslide. At that Denali and Jasmine began to pitch rocks too and moved down to a better vantage point.

Except for the regular hypnotic sound of stones crashing

and thudding, all else was still. The sun was bright, the air warm, and a red-tailed hawk circled overhead as Jasmine and Denali threw more rocks. I studied them, their determination to find the best rocks, their drive to throw them farther, and their childish exuberance in such simple and natural play.

I heard Ursula walk up behind me and felt her hands on my shoulders. "You know you're not teaching your kids good habits."

I shrugged, and before I could state my case she called out, "You guys need to be careful. This mountain can be quite dangerous."

Almost in unison the twins turned, annoyed at the caution. "Mom, we're fine, fine." They giggled and hurled more rocks downhill.

At my request, Ursula handed me a nearby rock. I rubbed it, grinning as if I held a gold nugget.

"Throw it, Daddy, throw it!" The twins looked back, laughed, and threw their own rocks, shoving and contending.

I smiled and looked down at the rock in my hand. Its roughness had scraped my palm, leaving dirt and sweaty flakes, yet I found the sensation comforting, soothing somehow. I looked up, grinning and nodding, and squeezed the stone hard. It felt cool and coarse and moist, and as I closed my eyes, listening to my children, I tightened my fingers around it. And when the stone's sharp edges stung my skin, even that sting felt like hope.

Printed in the United States
213273BV00002B/2/P

9 781608 300129